Crap: A Guide

Also available from Continuum

Crap:
A Guide to Politics

TERRY ARTHUR

continuum

Continuum International Publishing Group
The Tower Building, 11 York Road, London SE1 7NX
80 Maiden Lane, Suite 704, New York NY 10038

www.continuumbooks.com

First published 2007

British Library Cataloguing-in-Publication Data
A catalogue record for this book is available from the British Library.

ISBN: 0–8264–9139–1 (paperback)

Typeset by Kenneth Burnley, Wirral, Cheshire
Printed and bound in Great Britain by MPG Books Ltd, Bodmin, Cornwall

Contents

Foreword   vi
Acknowledgements   vii

Introduction   1

1 Newspeak Crap   4

2 Contradictory Crap   16

3 Meaningless Crap   25

4 Statistical Crap   37

5 Cheeky Crap   50

6 Illogical Crap   64

7 Misleading Crap   79

8 Ideological Crap   93

9 One Rule for Them Crap   108

10 Fashionable Crap   120

11 Economic Crap   137

12 Prolific Crap   153

Conclusion   170

Index of Names   171
Subject Index   175

Foreword

Perhaps we live in such a depressing political system these days because all politicians seem to agree with each other: and in agreeing with each other they all speak the same language, of crap. Mr Arthur's book brilliantly exposes not just the ludicrous and often meaningless way in which so many of our rulers speak, but also, in doing so, he reveals the confidence trick that is being played upon all of us. What characterizes so much politics these days is the utter absence of principle with which it is conducted. We live, for worse, in the era of the career politician. Soon it will be the exception rather than the rule to have ministers whose life has not taken the following path: PPE at Oxford (or something distressingly similar), then work as a special adviser, spin doctor or researcher, then the backbenches, then office. The question is not just how such people can possibly be acquainted with the realities of the people over whom they rule; it is how, with such an upbringing, they could have ever have hoped to speak a language the rest of us could understand, let alone take seriously.

Mr Arthur has presented us with a user's manual to politicians. Anyone who reads it will not merely laugh out loud, but will be armed against all future attempts by the political class to lie, obfuscate and prevaricate. To this end some philanthropist should pay for a copy to be sent into every household in the land. However, there is an even more serious point. The continuous theme of this excellent little book is about the evils of the state, and of the importance of keeping politicians out of our lives as far as possible. Time and again their destructiveness, but also their sheer incomprehension and incompetence, are demonstrated: and we are their victims. Nor is this a party political point. They are all at it. Socialists, of course – that is their *raison d'être* – but also so-called liberals and, of course, in the era of the blessed Dave, so-called Conservatives.

This book holds lessons for us all. It is a further pointer to the fact that we need to get tougher with our politicians, and to abjure them for the way in which they patronise us and insult our intelligence. They have got away with it for too long. We are not a bovine people (or worse, an ovine one) to be herded about obediently by people who are, in fact, our intellectual and moral inferiors. This book opens a new front against these self-aggrandising, destructive and too often maleficent people. May it not be the last.

Simon Heffer – Associate Editor, the *Daily Telegraph*

Acknowledgements

I am grateful to very many people for their help in making this book a reality, not least the politicos who provided the material, although I wish it were otherwise. They have unwittingly combined with family, friends and acquaintances in urging me to follow up on my 1975 effort.

I owe an enormous debt to my wife Clare who has provided infinite support and help and borne all my preoccupations without a cross word, as well as providing many suggestions. My PA Mrs Jackie Whincop has typed the best part of the whole book, at work and at home, from both manuscript notes and internet sites found by deciphering many of my obtuse scribbles.

My close friend David Rosser has been a wonderful personal editor, spending many days and weeks of analysis and discussion. His time, strategic comments, and detailed editing (as only a top quality English Master could have done) have all been immense.

Other direct help and encouragement in one form or another has come from my own family and innumerable friends (both personal and business). My mother has a walk on part in Chapter 12!

The Institute of Economic Affairs, in particular its Editorial and Programme Director Philip Booth, is responsible not only for the launch of the book (as it was in 1975) but also for encouraging me in the first place and for introducing me to my publisher Continuum Books.

Other think tanks have also been helpful in various ways, in particular The Mises Institute in the USA (Ludwig von Mises' *Human Action* has been my bible for several decades) and Civitas in the UK who provided the Appendix to Chapter 12.

At Continuum, Alexandra Webster not only persuaded her directors to adopt a dodgy-sounding enterprise, but also has been unfailingly helpful, reliable and (importantly) available throughout. Sarah Patel took on the marketing role with great gusto. Her success is about to be measured – except that we will never know how much she has been hampered or otherwise by the quality of the material she has had to work with – for which along with all other errors, omissions, and shoddy workmanship I am solely to blame.

Introduction

No man's life, liberty, or property are safe when the legislature is in session.

(Mark Twain)

The impetus for the original edition of this book (*95 per cent is Crap: A Plain Man's Guide to British Politics*) was twofold. Firstly I discovered in the early 1970s that a particular objective (to do with Trade Unions as I recall) was easily achievable by repealing a previous Act of Parliament whereas in fact a new Act was piled on top of the old one. Silly, but great for the political class. Secondly I read all the manifestos for *both* of the 1974 general elections and was appalled by the extent of the crap – explicable only by large dollops of both stupidity and vested interests. I did not vote in either election and have not voted since. A cop out? No, because whatever I do it has no chance whatsoever of affecting the result, so why say yes when you mean no?

Unrestrained voting for <u>unrestrained</u> government always ends in tears; it can never be better than the divine right of majorities and in practice becomes the divine right of Big Government – whoever you vote for, Big Government gets in. Some will veer slightly towards more warfare, others towards more (so-called) welfare. In other words we'll get <u>statism</u> in any case. The last hundred years has seen government spending (as a proportion of output) multiply by ten, to 50 per cent. One thing is certain; a repeat performance is impossible.

As I hope will become clear, we have fallen for a Left versus Right hoax. Warfare and Welfare are two sides of a coin called Bigness and indeed are friends not enemies. (I hope that, too, will become clear. Basically Welfare leads to protectionism rather than free trade, and if goods don't cross borders armies will, while Warfare brings a bigger and more intrusive role for government that is never relinquished thereafter.)

1

This book is a plea against both, in favour of Top versus Bottom where Top is small and Bottom is big. As Lord Acton said, power corrupts, and the damage caused by Big Government is enormous. Every opportunity should be taken to give discredit where discredit is due – which is most of the time. Big Government is bad for everybody – except for the political class, referred to in this book as politicos.

Three short appendices cover slightly more technical issues, respectively on global warming (Chapter 6), a vital but little-discussed drawback of 'public sector' entities (Chapter 8), and monopoly (Chapter 11).

Thank you for reading this book and I hope that you laugh a lot – until you cry.

The underlying approach remains true to the first edition (1975) – direct quotations with appropriate remarks, split into chapters according to the nature of the crap rather than the subject matter. The sources are similar too – Party Manifestos and Conferences plus news and comments picked up mainly from one newspaper, this time *The Times* instead of the *Guardian*. Both have strong statist leanings but *The Times* is more in tune with today's BGC – Big Government Conservatism.

This time I have occasionally peeped over the waters – particularly westward to the USA (the home of BGC) and the United Nations, and sometimes eastward to the European Union.

A new chapter is also required for this edition, namely 'One Rule for Them' – an offshoot of Cheeky Crap, whereby the politicos are blatant about the double standards between Them and Us.

To keep the book fairly compact, something has had to give, namely two chapters and a few organisations. Yes and No Crap and Useless Crap could fill many books but, like the politicos themselves, are essentially hot air. For example, in the first edition of this book we had Ted Heath telling us that his government will take 'whatever action is necessary' to do a host of things including conserving the nation's energy supplies; we now have Home Secretary John Reid telling us (in the *Sunday Telegraph*, 21 January 2007) that he will do exactly the same thing to resolve the mess that is the Home Office.

Looking at the minority parties, the British National Party and the Greens are strikingly similar, essentially fascist anti-trade home-grown foodies – the fastest way to join the third world. (The only good thing about the Green Party is its research document showing that the Lib Dems did not oppose the Iraq War.[1]) Communism was founded on ignorance and hasn't changed. UKIP is a self-confessed single issue party. (To anybody who wants smaller government, leaving the European Union is a no-brainer, but this book isn't about single-issue politics.)

The TUC and CBI, once proud corporatists regularly supping in Downing Street and governing by nods and winks and hints, have been sensibly sidelined; unfortunately corporatism (an alliance of Big Government and Big Business) hasn't. Instead, specific legislation and regulation, promoted as often as not by Big Business aiming to exclude competition by law, and governed by state regulators often masquerading as consumer champions, is the order of the day. It's ironic to think that Dr Gertrude Kelly, born in 1862 and one of the earliest feminists in the United States, considered the free market to be a cure for capitalism – by which she meant corporatism.

Are you ready? Then let's go.

---

1 Green Party press office briefing May 2004.

1

Newspeak Crap

'The new Labour project was founded on a brilliant understanding of the power of language to frame ideas: no government has been more careful in its choice of words, or more ruthless in its exploitation of them. Soon after coming to power, Tony Blair remarked: 'You really have to learn a whole new language.' He did more than that: he forged one. In his 1946 essay "Politics and the English Language", George Orwell complained: "In our time, political speech and writing are largely in defence of the indefensible

. . . thus political language had to consist largely of euphemism, question-begging and sheer cloudy vagueness." Compared with the politicians of our time, those of Orwell's era seem paragons of plain-speaking.

In his study of Blair's rhetoric, New Labour, New Language, Professor Norman Fairclough identified the feel-good, loaded buzzwords that adorn the Prime Minister's language: "reform", "young", "deliver", "tough", "renew". Mr Blair is a "people" person: the "people's peers", the "people's Princess". These words waft like verbal perfume throughout his discourse, whether or not they have any relevance or significance.

Mr Blair's is the language of togetherness and perhaps his most damaging legacy to political speech is the coupling of opposites:

social justice and economic dynamism, ambition and compassion, fairness and enterprise, traditional values in a modern setting.'

(Ben Macintyre, The Times, *15 September 2006)*

As we can see from Ben Macintyre's excellent lexicon (and this is only an excerpt), George Orwell's Newspeak remains very much with us. It began as a special language used by a totalitarian government to control thoughts and beliefs. It consisted of a relatively small number of phrases, often formed by sticking together two or more words almost randomly, to be used repeatedly, thus blocking out real language and any associated thought processes. Thought is dangerous to the politicos.

Today, the most overworked word is probably 'social' and its various derivatives, such as 'social justice' – as if there could be any other kind of justice!

A short list of my own favourites is appended to this chapter. In the meantime let the politicos pour forth.

The words 'liberty' and 'freedom' remain firmly in place as favourites for emasculation. In the first edition we had:

The new liberty, then, is the politics of regulated conflict.

(Professor Ralf Dahrendorf, Reith Lectures 1974)

And Roy Hattersley's contribution was to equate freedom with wealth:

The E.E.C., in giving increased economic strength to each member State, makes it more free, not less so.

(Roy Hattersley, Guardian, *4 January 1974)*

Roy, bless him, is still with us:

In a free society shareholders should not be insulated from the peaceful protest of individuals and groups who believe companies' activities to be undesirable. That is not an argument in favour of violence and intimidation. It is an assertion of the right to know who owns the companies that, to a greater or lesser degree, influence our daily lives.

(Roy Hattersley, The Times, *9 June 2006)*

You can find that out any time, Roy, because significant shareholdings must be fully disclosed. And if you want to protest, where would you do it – at a shareholders' meeting? Even shareholders have the right to freedom of association without nosy-parkers like you gate-crashing. Or is that what you call a free society? Freedom to trespass?

In the land of the free they're a bit iffy on free speech. Yes I know you shouldn't shout 'fire' in a crowded theatre (unless there is one) but that's a matter for sensible rules by property owners and the terms of admission. Here we're speaking, freely I hope, about restrictions on 'commercial speech':

> Since the 1940s, the US Supreme Court has recognized a class of 'commercial speech' that is afforded less protection under the First Amendment to the United States Constitution than 'non-commercial' or political speech.
>
> *(S.M. Oliva, Mises Institute, 6 July 2006)*

Great wheeze for the politicos. Margaret Beckett could take that on board (see Chapter 7).

We all think we understand liberty. But liberalism is different. Ming Campbell thinks it's all to do with leadership:

> **Real liberalism means leading public opinion not following it.**
> *(Sir Menzies Campbell, Liberal Democrats Conference, September 2006)*

And there was I, thinking it was all about letting people do their own thing.

'Fair' and 'fairness' also have staying power: In 1975 we had:

> **The last Conservative Government went a long way towards making it [the tax system] fairer. Higher personal allowances gave proportionately more help to the less well off taxpayers.**
> *(Conservative Party Election Manifesto, October 1974)*

As I said at the time, if that is fair, why weren't they fairer still? They could have taken all the money from the rich. (Ah, but that would be unfair, wouldn't it?)

At what point does soaking the rich become *un*fair? And of course high *earners* are often not at all rich. But that doesn't deter the politicos today any more than it did then, especially our Mingy:

> Those who can afford to make a greater contribution should do so . . .
>
> Income tax cuts for hard working people.
>
> The polluter paying the price.
>
> Taxing wealth, not work.
>
> Now this is the politics of substance.
>
> It's fairness in action.
> *(Sir Menzies Campbell, Liberal Democrats Conference, September 2006)*

So who will pay for these cuts? *Soft*-working people? People who don't work or don't work hard?

Oh, sorry, the polluter. And if by some unlikely chance the polluter is a hard-working person?

And where does wealth come in here? As far as I know, Mingo, you have *no* plans to tax 'wealth'. You are going to tax high *earners* (hardworking people), by not 'subsidizing' their pension contributions. So a tax relief is a 'subsidy'. So Government decides I should pay 50 per cent tax on my hard work except I can keep a bit more of *my* money if I save it in ways of which you approve, then that's a subsidy is it?

Having condemned Cameron's Tories as a 'substance free zone' (right on the button, that) what can you give us, Mingy?

The answer is a switch to socialism from Charles Kennedy's individualist leanings (well-hidden though they were):

> A fair Britain is one where progressive taxation, based on people's ability to pay, redistributes money from the richest to the poorest.
> *(Liberal Democrat Party Policy Statement, 8 September 2006)*

At least Labour jettisoned its Clause 4!

Most of this arises from woolly or nonsensical phrases beginning with the word 'social', with 'fairness' being interchangeable with the ever-present 'social justice'.

Cameroon Tories are full of such blather. And Dave the Vague doesn't let us down, still 'laying the foundations' of his party's 'house' after a decade in opposition:

> Laying the foundations – social responsibility.
>
> *(David Cameron, Conservative Party Conference, October 2006)*

Stick 'social' in front of a useful word and you're away. Social justice, social security, and so on. How about some of the habits of government? Social disasters, social break ups, social injustice, social theft, social engineering; they're all there up with the best.

One of his small minority of female speakers (slipping there, Dave) is content with a renewal of the old concept:

> We need real fresh thinking on Social Justice . . .
>
> *(Caroline Spelman, Conservative Party Conference, October 2006)*

Note the capital letters. Not to be outdone by Miliband's 'double devolution' of power (see later in this chapter) she has Two Capitals. And the resemblance doesn't end there – she's going local/communitarian. Indeed the title of her speech is 'Regenerating our communities is a social, not just a state, responsibility'.

Who on earth thinks it *is* a state responsibility – even in part, Caroline? (So why take our money?) I thought you were in touch with we the people (sorry, sheeple). No, clearly only with the chattering classes on the public sector payroll.

Back to the statutory two capitals:

> This has to change. We will roll up these fragmented resources into a Cohesion Fund and make repeat funding available to those projects which prove their worth.

> The politicians closest to their communities are local councillors who rub shoulders with their constituents daily.
>
> *(Caroline Spelman, Conservative Party Conference, October 2006)*

A Cohesion Fund. Financed by taxes from us of course. But private enterprise (with or without capitals) can already cohere. It has prices – those funny things that blurt out the relative worth of everything millions of times a day. Ever heard of them?

No, she's beyond redemption. *Social* Enterprise comes next, not private enterprise. Strange that, Carlo, because private enterprise is, in essence, exchange and trade (sorry, Social Exchange and Social Trade).

But Caroline is addicted to meddling, with our money. Count the capitals in her rousing finale:

> As the *Big Issue* says 'A Hand Up Not a Hand Out'.
> *(Caroline Spelman, Conservative Party Conference, October 2006)*

I beg to differ. I prefer a hand OUT – *your hand* out of *my pocket*, please. Will the Tories be any better? Here's a premonition of Miliband:

> We believe in devolving power down to the lowest level so that local people are given greater control over their own lives.
> *(Conservative Party Election Manifesto 2005)*

Droning, devolving, evolving, what does it matter; he who pays the piper calls the tune, except when the payer is the taxpayer:

> The Conservatives will liberate local government.
> *(Conservative Party Election Manifesto 2005)*

How? By giving local communities a 'greater say'. Does that mean reducing income tax and letting local councils decide on their own services and the taxes or other funds to pay for them? Can't be – you've already said you're going to reduce *council* taxes, not central government taxes. Can't have that. Anyway I thought you were abolishing Local Government (as per above) or at least by-passing it.

Silly me. When would a Government make itself smaller or cut out some of its tentacles?

Is David Miliband equal to this blatant plagiarism, with his 'double devolution' of power – all the way from Whitehall to town hall to local communities? (Go a step or two further and we'll be in free market territory – great. But he won't get beyond the town hall.)

Maybe he's got double vision. Whatever he's got he's another of these guys who hop from one cabinet post to another and start to prance around with new 'expertise' within days.

Already he's moved from double to treble:

> At the moment, we are living, Britons in the 21st century, as if there were three planets to support us when in fact we have only one. We are consuming the natural resources of three planets; burning the fossil fuel of three planets; pumping out enough carbon dioxide for three planets; yet we only have one planet to live on . . . that is why today I propose we adopt a new goal as a country: to aim to live as a nation within the limits that the environment can tolerate, One Planet Living.
>
> *(David Miliband, Labour Party Conference 2006)*

Will that be one planet's environment, or three, David?

Party chairman Hazel (Blather) Blears brings him down to planet Earth and gets back to the bread and butter of socialist newspeak:

> My mentor and inspiration Barbara Castle once said that 'socialism is about the quality of human relationships'.
>
> *(Labour Party Conference 2006)*

That'll be *poor* quality, I presume. Because socialism is about force. And in my book, *exchange* (hardly encouraged by socialism) is the fundamental social relation. Free speech and its natural consequence, free trade.

By the way, do you ever get called Hazy, Hazel? Just wondered.

And so it rolls on. This one, from Labour's 2005 Manifesto, must have been dreamed up by Michael Meacher whom we met in 1975 (and will meet again later):

> By 2010 we will ensure that all social tenants benefit from a decent, warm home with modern facilities.
>
> *(Labour Party Manifesto 2005)*

Stick the word 'social' in front for a decent warm homely feeling. Except that it really means 'government'. Of course 'social housing' began in the 1920s, reaching a peak of a quarter of all homes by 1979; it's still a very large number. Why have the poor social tenants got to wait a century for a warm home?

Also from the Labour Manifesto is this equally standard newspeak stuff, but it's new to me:

> Our goal is employment opportunity for all – the modern definition of full employment.
>
> *(Labour Party Manifesto 2005)*

With this 'modern' definition it looks pretty measly to 'raise the employment rate to 80 per cent'. Why not 100 per cent? Although I do see what you mean; there's a bit of a barrier for those outlawed from employment such as those who can't earn your imposed minimum wage, or can earn next to nothing in excess of your 'welfare' benefits – to say nothing of those in prison for victimless crimes like drug-taking.

The Tories are no different:

> We will end waiting lists as we know them.
>
> *(Conservative Party Manifesto 2005)*

'As we know them' being the operative phrase. But it's too late, boys. Labour's Manifesto said that – *and delivered*, as Nigel Hawkes pointed out in *The Times* of 3 February 2006:

> What's the difference between a queue and a waiting list? In the NHS, queues don't count.
> It emerged yesterday that a hospital in Sunderland had put thousands of patients in a 'queue' rather than a traditional waiting list as they waited – or queued – for follow-up appointments.

But Blair must have been off-message because a couple of months later, on 19 April, *The Times* reported that the Prime Minister admitted that the NHS was at a 'crunch point' but insisted he was still on course for an historic 'end to traditional waiting' by 2008.

The same Tory Manifesto doesn't know what to do about the Iraq war which the Tories sanctioned:

> Mr Blair misrepresented intelligence to make the case for war in Iraq, and failed to plan for the aftermath of Saddam Hussein's downfall . . .

> So we believe that Britain must remain committed to rebuilding Iraq and allowing democracy to take hold . . .
>
> *(Conservative Party Manifesto 2005)*

But he didn't 'misrepresent' intelligence, he *invented* it. And you just can't admit defeat, can you? For 'democracy' read 'civil war'.

The US Democrats are a carbon copy:

> Our overriding goals are the same as ever: . . .

> To promote democracy and freedom around the world, starting with a peaceful and stable Iraq . . .

> Democracy will not blossom overnight, but America should speed its growth by sustaining the forces of democracy against repressive regimes and by rewarding governments that work toward this end . . .

> Containing this massive threat [terrorism] requires American leadership of the highest order . . . and compels problem states to join and comply with international agreements and abandon their weapons programs.
>
> *(US Democratic Party Platform 2004)*

So with *our* weaponry, we're going to impose democracy by force: er, doesn't that rather defeat the object?

If anybody can show me a successful democracy created *before* the pillars of civilization are in place (rule of law, protection of minorities, separation of powers, private property rights etc) I'll eat my hat. In fact the fusion of two different words into one phrase 'democracy and freedom' is an excellent example of Newspeak. 'Freedom, *then* democracy' is a far more accurate depiction of reality. (And even then democracy begins to destroy freedom – see Chapter 5.)

And no joy from the Republicans in the shape of GWB:

Elections are vital, but they are only the beginning. Raising up a democracy requires the rule of law and protection of minorities and strong, accountable institutions that last longer than a single vote . . .

The Palestinian people have voted in elections, and now the leaders of Hamas must recognize Israel, disarm, reject terrorism, and work for lasting peace.

(George W. Bush, State of the Union Address, 31 January 2006)

Elections are the end, George, not the beginning, as you'll find out when the leaders of Hamas ignore you. Better get among 'em quick.

He's still on a roll in mid-2006:

America makes no distinction between the terrorists and the countries that harbor them. If you harbor a terrorist, you are just as guilty as the terrorists and you're an enemy of the United States of America.

(George W. Bush, speech at the graduation ceremonies of the US Military Academy at West Point, New York, 27 May 2006)

Or between a government and its subjects?

Don't know about you, George, but the most helpful definition of terrorism I have seen, which comes from Edward Herman, Emeritus Professor at the Wharton School of Business, Pennsylvania, is 'the use of force or the threat of force against civilian populations to achieve political objectives'. (I'd also treat conscripts as civilians.) Note that this doesn't rule out a government as a perpetrator. Interesting, that.

Also newly prominent is the issue of security. Back at home, before he got kicked out Charles Clarke had Hitler's Gestapo strategy:

I understand the quasi-constitutional objections of some in the other place to the idea that a British citizen should have an identity card whether they want it or not – that is the essence of their concern.

(Charles Clarke, House of Commons, 29 March 2006)

Quasi-constitutional; interesting expression, that. We the sheeple don't *really* mind your disrespect to 'the other place' (quasi no doubt) but can we assume that if we don't like an ID card you'll give us it for nowt and let us be free to throw it away?

I'm grateful to Alan Coren of *The Times* for relating a German newspaper story about a 'security camera' spying on the flat of the Chancellor Angela Merkel. As he says, George Orwell would be savouring it because in truth it's an *insecurity* camera. The newspaper said the filming of the flat (oh yes, the camera was filming) was like a scene from Big Brother. It could equally have said Hitler's Gestapo – or Stalin's Kremlin – or Clarke's stormtroopers.

Patricia Hewitt is not to be outdone:

> The Honourable Gentleman has fallen into precisely the trap that so much of the media have and that I warned against earlier; those are not sackings. The hospital is making difficult decisions because it has a serious financial deficit.
>
> *(Patricia Hewitt, Secretary of State for Health,*
> *House of Commons, 7 June 2006)*

The 'difficult decisions' included 150 redundancies. When is a sacking not a sacking? When you've sent somebody packing.

Just in case you think Newspeak is the preserve of the professional politicos, here's an example from one of our giant nationalized industries – Education. Here is a retired primary school teacher, Mrs Liz Beattie:

> Conference believes it is time to delete the word 'fail' from the educational vocabulary, to be replaced with the concept of 'deferred success'.
>
> *(Mrs Liz Beattie,*
> *Conference of the Professional Association of Teachers, July 2005)*

Enjoy your pension, Mrs B. It's time for me to have a break; or 'deferred writing' if you like.

Appendix: A selection of today's favourite newspeaks

Apartheid	existence of private sector (e.g. Educational Apartheid)
Authoritative	government-commissioned
Auto-enrolment	inertia selling
Civil (servant)	neither civil nor servile
Collateral damage	killing non-enemies
Commercial speech	unfree speech (USA)
Democracy	big coercive government
Downing Street	Prime Minister's lackeys
Economic patriotism	nationalism
Eminent domain	expropriation (USA)
Food miles (bad)	free trade
Food patriotism	food nationalism
Friendly fire	killing colleagues
Government funded	tax-payer funded
Independent	government-selected (e.g Bank of England Directors/Committee)
Legal tender	compulsory medium of exchange
Liberalism	theft
Market forces	voluntary cooperation
Mission creep	grotesque cost over-run
Price war	competition to serve customers
Public goods	stolen goods
Public v private	coercive v voluntary
Renewal	waste
Renewable	more waste
Service	placing in queue
Shock and awe	mass murder
Single payer	private sector banned (USA)
Social housing	sink estates
Social justice	theft
Social pollution	obesity
Social responsibility	coercion
Social security	insecurity
Stakeholders	slaves
Surgical strike	killing the enemy
Sustainable	unsustainable
Ticket tout	retailer
Trafficking	selling
War	The Health of the State
War on . . .	persecution (e.g. war on terror or drugs)
Wellness	illness

2

Contradictory Crap

The principal failing was in the sailing
And the bellman, perplexed and distressed,
Said you'd think that at least when the wind blew due East
The ship wouldn't travel due West.

(Lewis Carroll, The Hunting of the Snark*)*

As the politicos have become bolder with their blather, cheek, spin, and lies, outright contradictions are getting harder to spot. Some of them have been commandeered into Newspeak; many examples of Newspeak involve words used to mean the opposite of the norm, like freedom, fairness, and security, as we have seen in Chapter 1.

But some contradictions will never die. The classic from the first edition came from Jeremy Thorpe's Liberal Party:

> The first is to re-create in our society and in our political institutions a loyalty to 'the general good', to which all sectional and partisan interests, however inherently worthy, must be subordinate . . .

> Liberals believe in the supremacy of the individual.
> *(Liberal Party Election Manifesto February 1974)*

The supremacy of the subordinate individual!

In those days, one of the major vehicles for subordination was the Social Contract, which featured very heavily in 1975. Here's Jim Callaghan:

> Everyone is involved in the Social Contract – Government, industry, trades unions, local government – every citizen has his part to play . . .
> *(James Callaghan, Labour Party Conference 1974)*

The whole meaning of a contract requires all signatories to – well – sign it!

We have something similar from David (Two Brains) Willetts on the new buzz phrase of social responsibility:

> We are focusing on the authentic Conservative theme of responsibility. That must mean individual responsibility. But it goes beyond that. It must be social responsibility. It includes responsibility to one's family, to one's profession, and to one's neighbourhood . . .
>
> *(David Willetts, Conservative Party Conference 2006)*

Nothing you mention here, Two Brains, 'goes beyond' *individual* responsibility – to one's family, profession, neighbourhood, and so on. Just like feeding the dog, these are all good examples of obligations *within* individual responsibility, not *beyond* it. The frustrating part is that, unlike Miliband and a host of others, you *know* that.

And if you know someone is responsible, David, you can cut them a little slack. We the sheeple will take it all on if you give us just half of our money back. Now that's generous, you must admit.

We have also already seen several flashy genuflections from central government towards 'devolution'. The Lib Dems are the arch-contortionists here:

> We will free local councils from many of the stifling controls of central government so that they can innovate and deliver services that meet local people's real needs. Councils will become genuinely accountable to their local communities rather than being agents of Whitehall.
>
> *(Liberal Democrats Election Manifesto 2005)*

Good idea. But you forgot to say this bit: 'And the only way to do this is to allow them to collect their own revenue in a way that meets local people's real needs'. Is there any chance of that? Not on your Nellie:

> The Council Tax penalises pensioners and people on low incomes, who pay a far higher proportion of their income in Council Tax than the very rich. A Local Income Tax is based very simply on the ability to pay.
>
> *(Liberal Democrats Election Manifesto 2005)*

They don't have the field to themselves though. Labour can drill down even further:

> New powers for parish councils to deal with anti-social behaviour . . .
>
> Not a new tier of neighbourhood government, but new powers over the problems that confront them when they step outside their front door – issues like litter, graffiti and anti-social behaviour. That is why we will offer neighbourhoods a range of powers from which they can choose . . .
>
> *(Labour Party Manifesto 2005)*

Not a new tier; just a parish council with new powers. In any case, the problems of public streets are in a different tier altogether from those in private streets. Re-privatize the streets? (See also Chapter 10.)

Back in the first edition, *Guardian* journalist Adam Raphael was soft on crime:

> The Rehabilitation of Offenders' Act answers a real need. It allows certain offenders who have gone straight for a period of years to respond truthfully that they had never been convicted of a criminal offence.
>
> *(Adam Raphael,* Guardian, *15 December 1974)*

Even though they had!

The climate now, typified by John (Bull) Reid, wants to brand suspects for ever. But our John has a soft spot for victims:

> People want to know that the government is on the side of the victim, not protect-ing the criminal. That's fine by me, because it's this party, and has always been

this party, that's on the side of the decent, hard-working majority in our country . . . That's why I am going to introduce a Community Payback scheme . . .

(John Reid, Labour Party Conference 2006)

Community Payback, not victim payback – and no doubt pay into your back-pocket, John. This theme – tearful about victims, getting perpetrators to clean a street (no doubt miles away from the victim) – is supported by all the politicos. It's as good an example as any of the great divide between them and the people. When is somebody going to tell us what's wrong with compensation for victims – yes, plain vanilla compensation? As it was before Government got in on the act.

Victims? What victims? Says our Top Cop:

London is returning to an era of neighbourliness and low crime in which people are happy to leave their front doors open, according to the country's most senior policeman . . .

But the gaffe-prone commissioner's claims appear to be contradicted by local crime figures and his own force's crime prevention advice.

(Sir Ian Blair, Commissioner of Metropolitan Police, as reported in
The Times, *21 August 2006)*

Don't suppose Sir Ian leaves *his* door unlocked, do you? (Unless he has a permanent posse on guard, at our expense.)

What do the Tories think? Ignoring the evidence of the NHS, where more means less, they want more coppers:

5,000 extra police a year. Less paperwork and political correctness.
(Conservative Party Manifesto 2005)

5,000 extra police officers *per year*. Now that's going some. And less paperwork – very funny. And why only *less* political correctness? How much do you want?

The pace doesn't really slacken at their conference, where Cameron and Osborne run the show and ensure that lower taxes don't get a look in. Having rightly berated Gordon Brown for his tax raid on pensions (see Chapter 9) George is not going to do anything about it:

> We will share the proceeds of growth between the lower taxes this country needs and the increases in spending on public services every government should provide . . .
>
> As Mrs Thatcher herself said . . . 'I am not prepared ever to go on with tax reductions if it meant unsound finance.'
>
> She was right on that as on so much else.
>
> *(George Osborne, Conservative Party Conference 2006)*

Part of the so much else being selling off lots of public services (that 'every government should provide') so as to reduce taxes. And what her 1979 manifesto said was: 'We shall cut income tax at all levels'.

The day before that Chris Grayling was disagreeing with professional engineers about energy:

> Today we are launching a new website – howgreenisyourcar.co.uk
>
> You can see its homepage on the screen behind me. It contains the league tables that the Government will not publish. It also contains environmental information about every car currently on sale in the UK.
>
> *(Chris Grayling, Conservative Party Conference 2006)*

I visited the site, Chris. It turns out to be based entirely on CO_2 emissions. But what about the energy costs which you politicos are always banging on about? Over the whole process from manufacture to disposal, the Toyota Prius (top of its class in your table) appears to cost six times as much in energy as a Ford Escort (according to *Professional Engineering*, 12 April 2006).

Roads are one thing; railways are another:

> I want rail professionals running our railways. It is time Whitehall stopped playing the fat controller.
>
> *(Chris Grayling, Conservative Party Conference 2006)*

All politicos want to meddle with the railways, including the MPs' Transport Committee, which *The Economist* of 27 May 2006 called 'pugilistic', pointing out that the Committee's view that prices are too high is hard to reconcile with the fact that more people than ever are paying them.

At the time none of us knew that in 2005 Alistair Darling made a secret deal with Britain's biggest train company, First Capital Connect, to *double* fares on certain routes 'as the cheapest way of reducing overcrowding', as revealed by *The Times* of 29 June 2006. Stand up those who are surprised at such duplicity. Later, in January 2007, the head of Railways at the Department of Transport said that rail commuters travelling at peak periods should expect to stand even if they have paid £5,000 for an annual season ticket. At least we can see that private enterprise is *not* running the railways.

And of course the taxpayer boards every train, or at least his money does, with a cool £5 billion or so p.a.

David Cameron wants to meddle and deny it:

> Food was not a state responsibility but a social responsibility, Mr Cameron said . . .
>
> The Government should investigate ways to improve cooking skills, knowledge and principles of nutrition, following through on Jamie Oliver's campaign on school food, and considering measures to control the marketing of food to children, not just through television advertising but with texts, promotions and sponsorship.
>
> *(David Cameron, speaking to the Slow Food Movement, as reported in* The Times, *2 December 2006)*

Not a state responsibility, but the state will treat it as one!

The politicos argue of course, but only on HOW to meddle. Libby Purves is a prime example:

> Labour's infuriating instinct to meddle in our lives provides the Tory leader with an ideal opportunity.
>
> *(Libby Purves,* The Times, *20 June 2006)*

So far so good, until she elevates herself to philosopher status:

> Yet when I was thinking, philosophically, about the diversity of governments across the world – some save you from starving and some don't, some are strict on traders, some slack – I tried to formulate a rule of thumb about when wise governments should interfere between citizens in non-violent, non-criminal matters . . .

> Protection, it seemed to me, is needed in areas of financial com-
> plexity in which one side has professional expertise and the other
> does not . . .
>
> Meanwhile, HMG scolds about fat children and bans us from
> selling private property without paying an expensive and half-
> trained 'inspector'. Where's the philosophy?
>
> *(Libby Purves, The Times, 1 August 2006)*

Philosophy? A little knowledge of history would help. For at least two
decades Government regulation of pensions has become more and
more stifling to the point of suffocation. The same goes for financial
services generally, where regulations make it simple to borrow and
tortuous to save.

F.A. Hayek *was* a philosopher. What you should bone up on, Libby,
is Hayek's idea that 'members of the opinion-moulding class' (including journalists) are predominantly 'dealers in second hand ideas'.

Ken Livingstone, the Mayor of London, has a simple philosophy.
He wants to rule by fear and if contradictions get in the way who gives
a monkey's? The global warming hype is a godsend, but Mick Hume
has him taped:

> It was not the fear of terrorism making commuters sweat on the
> London Underground during this week's heatwave. Especially
> when we read the front-page warning from Ken Livingstone that,
> because of global warming (not to be confused with a dilapidated
> transport system), we are 'getting to the point where if a train
> breaks down in those conditions you could have serious loss of life'.
> As the sun went in last autumn, you may recall, Ken told us to
> expect a winter freeze to match 1963 – the worst in 200 years – with
> 'quite severe loss of life'. Whatever the weather, it seems there is
> no situation so bad that it cannot be made to feel worse by a few
> sunny words from the Miserabilist of London.
>
> *(Ken Livingstone, reported by Mick Hume, The Times, 7 July 2006)*

Many thanks to Mick Hume for this example. Miserabi*list* is spot on
– he's not miserable but he wants *us* to be; then he can say he's
stepping in to save us all.

Like John Kerry, over the pond:

John Kerry, John Edwards and the Democratic Party will send a clear message to every man and woman in our armed forces: We guarantee that you will always be the best-led, best-equipped and most respected fighting force in the world. You will be armed with the right weapons, schooled in the right skills, and fully prepared to win on the battlefield. You will never be sent into harm's way without enough troops for the task, and never asked to fight a war without a plan to win the peace. You will never be given assignments which have not been clearly defined and for which you are not professionally trained.

(US Democratic Party Platform 2004)

Super duper; the best deserve the best, don't they John?

Senator Kerry, speaking to a group of students in California on Monday, said: 'You know, education, if you make the most of it, you study hard, you do your homework and you make an effort to be smart, you can do well. If you don't, you get stuck in Iraq.'

(Reported in The Times, *2 November 2006)*

And this time they'll have to do just that – get stuck in:

In the long run, the most realistic way to protect the American people is to provide a hopeful alternative to the hateful ideology of the enemy – by advancing liberty across a troubled region . . .

In earlier operations, political and sectarian interference prevented Iraqi and American forces from going into neighborhoods that are home to those fueling the sectarian violence. This time, Iraqi and American forces will have a green light to enter these neighborhoods . . .

(George Bush, Address to the nation, 10 January, 2007)

Advancing liberty, as Lew Rockwell points out in a Mises Institute article the next day, by continued military occupation, threats, violence, martial law, and death, this time without caution or wincing.

Whatever aspects of liberty remain in the land of the free, it's not free trade.

Oh yes it is:

> We will make it a priority to knock down barriers to free, fair and
> balanced trade so other nations' markets are as open as our own . . .
>
> *(US Democratic Party Platform 2004)*

Oh no it isn't.

> We will effectively enforce our trade laws protecting against
> dumping, illegal subsidies, and import surges that threaten
> American jobs.
>
> *(US Democratic Party Platform 2004)*

At least the UK had proper, unilateral, free trade – once upon a time.
The USA didn't – not since the Boston Tea Party anyway. Flash
Gordo Brown prefers the USA model, as we shall see.

But not in this chapter – he's a little too devious for that.

3

Meaningless Crap

At Prime Minister's Questions Tony Blair has been quite crazy. I am a latecomer to the 'Blair is mad' theory, but I am beginning to see what it's all about. Look at this from last week:

> David Cameron (paraphrased): Will automatic deportation of foreign nationals apply to those 'convicted of an imprisonable offence', as the Prime Minister said two weeks ago; actually imprisoned, as he said last week; or serving a 'significant' jail term, as the Home Secretary said? Which is it? Read the Prime Minister's reply slowly: 'It is exactly as I explained when I first answered the Right Hon. Gentleman. It applies only to people who have gone to prison, which is why we are talking about foreign prisoners.
>
> 'If, for example, someone is sent to prison for a very short space of time and they have been in this country for a long period of time, then the presumption of automatic deportation would not apply, but in the vast bulk of cases, as has been explained, there will be an automatic presumption to deport, and the vast bulk of those people will, indeed, be deported . . .'
>
> *(Alice Miles,* The Times, *24 May 2006)*

Thank you, Alice, for one of many examples of Tony's ramblings. One day somebody will write a whole book about them. So filling a chapter from a load of politicos is not too difficult. Meaningless crap is a less harmful version of Newspeak, not so much to control as to obscure, distract, or keep a rival off the podium, by doodling with words and their order in any manner of ways. You get the picture.

In 1975, this chapter started off with a quote from Michael Heseltine:

> When I said on 12th February that it [the provision of more finance for the hovertrain project] was still being considered I was not lying, but giving a global answer.
>
> *(Michael Heseltine,* Guardian, *10 September 1973)*

I'm no nearer to understanding that now than when I first read it. Hezza is still around, heading a Cities Task Force for the Tories. Global cities, no doubt.

Nothing global about Peter Hain, once a student who dug up grass cricket pitches, but by 1974 a Liberal concerned with grass roots:

> Britain is becoming ungovernable, and Liberals must continue to press for a different style of politics as the only way to restore a governable situation and arrest the tide. People have to become involved in political life once more, and the only possible coalition is one in which people are united at the grass roots.
>
> *(Peter Hain, Liberal Party Conference 1974)*

To which I asked 'Now why didn't we think of that before?'

Always illiberal, Hain eventually joined the Labour Party and climbed the greasy pole to join the devolution bandwagon. As meaningless as ever, here's a typical current offering:

> We are reinvigorating local government – with extra powers and spending responsibilities. Because devolution of power must not stop at a national level. And because councillors know best how to serve their local communities.
>
> We're introducing a fairer system of local taxation, based on the real value of your property – with a generous system of reliefs for those on low incomes.
>
> *(Peter Hain, Labour Party Conference 2006)*

Wouldn't you think that councillors who know how best to serve would also know how best to *tax*? No doubt that's off limits, eh?

Yet Power for the People is king:

> Widening access to power is as important as widening access to wealth and opportunity.
>
> *(Labour Party Manifesto 2005)*

Sometimes you really think they believe their own guff. Let's go from Local to Global:

Official figures report that 6,600 Iraqis suffered violent deaths in July and August, a 13 per cent increase on the previous two months. It is the bitterest of ironies that in the aftermath of an invasion, justified in the name of liberation, the chief expert on torture for the United Nations, Manfred Nowak, describes the current situation as 'out of control', saying that the use of torture by the security forces, militias and the insurgency may be 'worse than in the times of Saddam Hussein' . . .

Against this background the UN, with full and unrestricted backing from the European Union, has to take over running the country.

(Dr Toby Dodge, Reader in International Politics at Queen Mary University of London, reported in The Times, *5 October 2006)*

Sorry if it's offensive to call this meaningless. Well no, I'm not, because that's what it is. It's an outlandish fairy-tale. This is the UN we're talking about, a body regularly and rightly lambasted as corrupt (remember the oil-for-food scandal?), which has been powerless to stop over 300 wars, and which is facing fresh accusations of bureaucratic incompetence after the disclosure that renovation costs for its vast New York head-quarters have rocketed to nearly £1 billion. We have all learned that no outside agency can take over the running of Iraq, let alone one that tolerates sexual abuses by its peacekeepers and aid workers (as it has been found to do by a Save the Children Fund investigation). I've met some mad professors in my time but really . . . And this is the organization which expects us to trust its reports on global warming – especially the highly doctored 'summaries for policy-makers'.

Is that what taxpayer funds do for us?

You can't win. You pay for useless global bodies and you pay for the horrors of globalization:

[Globalization] brings great benefits but also has the capacity to tear societies apart. One of the reasons why we have adopted a more egalitarian tax policy is not that rich people are bad – indeed they are necessary for wealth creation – but that without some pooling of resources and risk we cease to exist as a society in any meaningful way.

(Dr Vince Cable, Liberal Democrats Conference 2006)

Meaningfully meaningless, then? What's really going on here, Dr Cable? What are you a doctor of, by the way? I'm told you're an economist but if you're genuine you'll be scrapping the minimum wage (see Chapter 6) and I see no sign of that.

Anyway, good that you see the 'need' for rich people although I wouldn't put it quite like that myself. But are you saying that the greedy and jealous may want to live off the back of other people – so you're thieving from the rich to stop them being lynched, or what? And the 'globalization' reference is a little Delphic too, if not Heseltinian – you'd think it would join people together. And you'd also think that an economist might know that international trade (as a proportion of the total) was at least as large a century ago as it is now.

In fact we may never get back to that level again. Not if Margaret Beckett is right anyway; as a prelude to the Stern Report she sees 'wars fought over limited resources'. The cause? Climate change. No crap – she is absolutely right that nationalism leads to war. Once governments get in on actions taken to control the planet then war will indeed result although she doesn't see the causality.

Far more typical is her parliamentary performance on 13 June 2006. Ann Treneman gives us a flavour:

> It is Margaret Beckett's particular gift that she is able to say nothing and everything at the same time. It really is a wonder to behold although, obviously, if you are actually looking for an answer it would make you want to scream. But, as pure evasion theatre, Mrs Beckett really cannot be beaten. She should have her own TV quiz called 'What Do You Think Margaret Is Saying?' . . .

The WHAT DO YOU THINK MARGARET IS SAYING? *Show*

?

'The European Union itself is entering into a period of an increased degree of mutual confidence' she said, her incredibly orange lips moving into a very thin smile.

(Margaret Beckett, reported by Ann Treneman, The Times, 14 June 2006)

One does wonder about the fairer sex occasionally. I suppose Sarah Teather is rather new on the block but how far does this advance the sum of human knowledge?

We need an education system that knows what every teacher knows and wants what every parent wants, a system which serves the individual, not the state.

(Sarah Teather, Liberal Democrats Conference 2006)

Now I grant you the last half Sarah, but if you believe the 'system should know what every teacher knows' you're talking crap. And state education has had ample time – many generations of kids – to show that it can serve the individual. In fact I'm bending over backwards to call it meaningless – it's not quite innocent enough for that.

And the big gun, Ruth Kelly, tells Parliament that some guy called Dave . . .

Wanted 'public money spent on private independent schools' – that sounds like vouchers to me. It is anything to anyone . . .

(Ruth Kelly, House of Commons, 27 March 2006)

These privately educated people (most of the Cabinet went to private schools or grammar schools of course) should really learn to articulate a little better.

Dr Rowan Williams went to Cambridge to learn this:

We need, not human words that will decisively capture what the Word of God has done and is doing, but words that will show us how much time we have to take in fathoming this reality, helping us turn and move and see, from what may be infinitesimally differ-ent perspectives, the patterns of light and shadow in a world where the Word's light has been made manifest.

(Dr Rowan Williams, Archbishop of Canterbury, reported in The Times, 26 June 2006)

Don't let *him* anywhere near a school, faith or otherwise.

And here is Sir Ian Blair who went to Oxford:

> Sir Ian mused that 'We want a 6 July police service, not a 7 July police service. However, we can't have that to which 6 July aspired without understanding 7 July. Moreover . . . I believe that we can't now have either 7 July or 6 July without risks like that of 22 July.' At the conclusion of this confusing account, he stated: 'I believe it should be you, not me, who decides what kind of police we want'.
>
> *(Reported in* The Times, *26 June 2006)*

Thanks a lot indeed. And thank you Tim Hames, whose article containing these gems was headed 'Beware the folly of clever men in power'. Rather like Hayek's notion mentioned in Chapter 2, where Libby Purves gave us such a good example.

Not much point in asking Sir Ian to scuttle across to North Wales:

> A violent crime is recorded only once. The stranger, public places, licensed premises, under the influences are all aspects of the same crime. One violent crime could therefore be counted in any or all four indicators, and of course none of the indicators.
>
> The indicators will cause duplication in counting violent crimes as they are not exclusive, but this in no way affects the number of violent crimes recorded. Each violent crime aggrieved as a victim/ offender relationship field. Where this is not a known person (family, friend, acquaintance, etc) the offender is termed a Stranger.
>
> *(Alan Hamilton, reporting a North Wales Police answer to a local Council,* The Times, *17 February 2006)*

We certainly have some serious issues in education. Is Labour equal to the task? Not if their manifesto is anything to go by:

> We will entrench high expectations for every child.
>
> *(Labour Party Manifesto 2005)*

And no doubt entrench the resulting disappointment.

Even though:

> A strong, effective governing body is essential to the success of every school and governors must be given support to help them play this role.
>
> *(Labour Party Manifesto 2005)*

So are we going to have bursars and proper reports and accounts? Oh no, not *that* effective.

Enough of schools. Time we grew up into responsible citizens:

> We Liberal Democrats are different. Here is exactly what we'll do.
>
> *(Sir Menzies Campbell, Liberal Democrats Conference 2006)*

Having told us that total taxes will not go up (except via his unleashed Local Authorities) Ming clearly hasn't a clue about what to do with the *current* tax loot:

> We need to spend that money more wisely . . .
>
> Reforms must be thought through . . .
>
> Stability can be only achieved through long term planning.
>
> *(Sir Menzies Campbell, Liberal Democrats Conference 2006)*

Can we have our money back – or at least all the excess Gordo took without thinking anything through – while we twiddle our thumbs waiting for your master plan? That might even earn the epithet of 'liberalism'.

Mind you, he has a real rival in Dave the Vague, with his trite 'Compassionate Conservatism' and 'There is such a thing as society – but it's not the same as the state' rejoinder to a quote from Margaret Thatcher taken entirely out of context.

Entirely *in* context, I'm afraid, is Dave's repeated vacuity, such as this:

> So our response [to public services], based on our philosophy of social responsibility, is to say to our nurses, doctors, teachers:
>
> Yes you should meet higher standards, yes you should give your patients and your pupils more.

> But we're not going to tell you how to do it.
> You are professionals.
> We trust in your vocation.
> So in a Conservative Britain, professional responsibility will provide the answer to rising expectations in the NHS and schools.
>
> *(David Cameron, Conservative Party Conference 2006)*

If you're wondering why this is meaningless, it's because it is a fairy tale to match that of Dr Toby Dodge. Do you mean those doctors whose pay has doubled since 1997? Or those junior surgeons who are walking out halfway through operations because of rules over the hours they work? They are routinely downing scalpels before procedures are complete, to comply with the European Union's controversial Working Time Directive (as reported in the *Sunday Telegraph*, 12 November 2006).

Is it any wonder that this guy has a Policy Review entitled 'Beginning Intellectual Renewal'?

But sometimes he's rigorous. Oh yes:

> A real commitment to rigour from the centre then needs to be underpinned by greater freedom for schools to manage their own affairs and a greater diversity of schools for parents to choose between.
>
> *(David Cameron, article in the* Daily Telegraph, *27 July 2005)*

Rigour? De rigueur is what interests Dave the Vague. Guess the title of this article. Would you believe 'We need to end woolly thinking and focus instead on literacy and discipline'?

It hardly needs saying that the incumbents are no better.

Here's Tessa the culture vulture:

> And they [people] look to the Labour party to ensure opportunity is there for all and that there is help for those who struggle to get on by themselves.
>
> Take the digital revolution . . .
>
> And here we see the limit of the market and the protective power of government: to ensure that those who are elderly, isolated or have disabilities are not left behind.
>
> *(Tessa Jowell, Labour Party Conference 2006)*

Funny that, Tessa. I might be dyslexic but I see the limit of government and the protective power of the market. Let's have a vote.

Tessa's colleague Yvette Cooper (Minister of State, Housing and Planning) knows all about 'sustainable communities':

> Sir John Egan was commissioned in April 2003 by my Right Hon. Friend the *Deputy Prime Minister* to review the skills and training required to deliver sustainable communities. His 'Review of Skills for Sustainable Communities' was published in April 2004. His key recommendation was the formation of a national centre to drive forward a new integrated approach to skills development.
>
> The Government responded by establishing the Academy for Sustainable Communities (ASC) to improve the skills, knowledge and behaviours needed to deliver and maintain sustainable communities across the country.
>
> *(Yvette Cooper, House of Commons 3 July 2006)*

Hey diddle diddle.

She's a fabulous deliverer is our Yvette. 'Sustainable communities' and now 'outcomes':

> The neighbourhood management pathfinder programme is subject to a comprehensive national evaluation. The most recent report (Neighbourhood Renewal Unit Research Report 23) stated that neighbourhood management is capable of delivering better outcomes for deprived areas, and is a valuable tool that deserves to be developed and adopted more widely. Planned future research will address more directly the costs and benefits of the programme, though it should be noted that quantifying the impact of neighbourhood management is made harder because it works by influencing existing service providers rather than delivering and funding new services and projects directly.
>
> *(Yvette Cooper, House of Commons, 29 June 2006)*

She sounds really clever, don't you think? After all, she's from Oxbridge too. She can certainly deliver words by the bucket load but the order doesn't seem to matter too much.

Steve Byers also has a reputation as a clever bugger. Clever cheat anyway, with his dodgy dossiers on British Rail and Rover, to name only two. He's a stayer, this chap:

> This will be a key moment in British politics because it will set out the boundaries and scope of the welfare state for the foreseeable future. Spending allocations for the remainder of this Parliament will be decided, and it will effectively write many of the key elements of Labour's manifesto for the next general election . . .
>
> That is why it is so important that we renew ourselves as new Labour. Many of our critics have failed to understand its strengths and appeal. It was never just a rebranding exercise but was a well-thought-out, robust and policy-dominated approach aiming to meet problems of our time with new solutions that remained true to the party's long established values.
>
> *(Stephen Byers,* The Times, *28 August 2006)*

These politicos have so much stamina. I'm nearly spent, with all this hot air. But I get a second wind when 'global warming' comes on the scene. What a boon it is for *them* versus *us*. And how they spout.

Schools are great places to learn the currently fashionable tosh about global warming of course. As Ann Treneman has shown, Margaret Beckett could fill this chapter on her own, so the following is a slightly paraphrased version of part of her exchange on Kyoto with John Humphreys on 28 March 2006.

> We're not giving up on target (to cut CO_2 emissions by 20 per cent) but 2010 is no longer achievable. We can't set out the precise path to it today.

> We can move a long way. This is not the last word on it. We have drawn together many proposals in our review published today; but a lot more is to come.

> We are going to better the Kyoto targets.

Re Rowan Williams' comment that our lifestyles are 'killing the poor', we need action on a number of levels. Government will push but we must see the views of poorer countries.

Unchecked growth would argue for substantially more aviation by 2020 than the doubling that we envisage.

No government is doing more.

Both public and private sectors must act. The public sector will promote a communications programme and each of us should look at the way we use energy.

(Margaret Beckett, BBC Radio, Today *programme, 28 March 2006)*

It is worth elaborating a little on Rowan Williams's comments earlier in the programme. Or is it? He said, *inter alia*, that the lifestyles of those contributing the most to global warming were 'profoundly immoral' and that politicians would 'face heavy responsibility before God' if they failed to act to control climate change. (Let God move us all to another planet, I say.)

And how immoral would the Kyoto agreement be if Fredrik Segerfeldt (Swedish author of *Water for Sale*) is correct in his estimate that one year of 'no Kyoto' could banish 12 million deaths a year from water-related diseases (see also Chapter 8)?

David Davis claims that this has always been Tory territory:

There can be no more Conservative idea than the conservation of nature.

(David Davis, Conservative Party Conference 2006)

The next day, Peter Ainsworth (Shadow Environment Secretary) has a better idea:

Second, we need a new body, independent of politics, to monitor the changing science of climate change, assess the risk, and make recommendations about the action government needs to take.

(Peter Ainsworth, Conservative Party Conference 2006)

Independent of politics – although set up by politicians. Isn't that some kind of oxymoron? Sir Nicholas Stern has already been there and done that – he wrote a 'Review on the Economics of Climate Change' for Gordon Brown, and resigned after being cold-shouldered.

How about consulting some of the 19,000 scientists who disagree with the cosy UK political consensus, as cited in a letter to the *Sunday Telegraph* of 7 May 2006 (also see Chapter 6)? Now that *would* be independent.

Dream on. It's time for a rest anyway.

4

Statistical Crap

Official statistics are just one more variant of Government obfuscation.
(Benjamin Disraeli)

And what a huge variant they have become since 1975, never mind Disraeli's days – which is why we need a health warning before dipping into what is now a cesspit. We all know that there are lies, damned lies, and statistics. My main purpose in this chapter is not to spout figures that refute those of the politicos, although that happens too when I'm confident that you'll see why. Otherwise, one risks playing into the hands of people like Gordon Brown, whose career is based on statistical gerrymandering: first formulate your argument and then search for some numbers (policy-based evidence rather than evidence-based policy, as John Kay puts it in the *Financial Times* of 4 September 2006). Or search for some numbers and then find an argument that they support, then discard or use according to taste.

The main aim here is to question the *purpose* of the statistics quoted. For statistics to be helpful, *there needs to be a clinical theory as well*. Preferably, the theory should be there *first*, as a *logical* hypothesis.

Furthermore it is dangerous for politicos to be involved at all – especially in selecting the topics to be investigated; investigations cost money and politicos' access to that is far too easy! An excellent example of that is the search for a link between mobile phones and cancer discussed at the end of this chapter.

During the 1970s, the price of an average basket of goods rose by a phenomenal 250 per cent (or 12.5 per cent per year), so 'inflation' (as measured by the Retail Prices Index, RPI) was a big issue and the trick of the Government was to raise taxes, *not in the RPI*, and subsidize the prices which *are* in the RPI. Many of the great and the good were fooled but not the then Chancellor, Denis Healey. Or was he?

> The average family in this country is now getting 85p a week off its
> food bills because of the food subsidies we are paying . . .
>
> *(Denis Healey, Labour Party Conference 1974)*

My main newspaper of the day, the *Guardian*, had shown him the
way:

> Slash indirect taxes – or subsidise housing and food – to hold the
> Retail Price Index down. Raise income tax steeply.
>
> (Guardian *Leader, 7 December 1973*)

Magic! More accurately, a confidence trick. Today, Gordon Brown is a
top rank con-man, making price inflation look about a half of the true
number when higher taxes are taken into account. (Brown's spree
raised taxes by well over 80 per cent in eight years – comfortably 50 per
cent over and above his CPI inflation.) Recently he pulled off a similar
trick with a similar effect; he jettisoned the Retail Prices Index (RPI)
which was looking a bit too sprightly, in favour of the Consumer Prices
Index (CPI) which has far less exposure to housing costs. At present,
these two tricks together make price inflation appear to be only about
a quarter of its true value. Also, the shopping baskets chosen for these
indexes are highly dubious and affect different groups in different
ways; if the *Daily Telegraph* had it right on 5 December 2006, living
costs are rising by 9 per cent a year for pensioners – *ignoring* the tax
trick above – while the CPI shows less than 2.5 per cent.

Similar manipulations are made for GDP (Gross Domestic
Product) where low numbers for price inflation feed straight through
into high numbers for growth. GDP numbers themselves are subject
to huge margins of 'error', perhaps as much as 10 per cent in any
year.[1] This kind of 'error' makes growth figures so wild that they are
quite simply 'not fit for purpose' (there is *no* purpose other than for
government to spew them out).

Which again leads directly to Flash Gordon:

> Britain is today experiencing the longest period of sustained
> economic growth since records began in the year 1701.
>
> *(Gordon Brown's Budget Speech, 16 March 2005)*

---

1 Philipp Bagus, Mises Institute, 17 August 2006.

This must rank as one of the most crass remarks ever made by a serious politician. Is he asking us to believe that GDP growth calculations 300 years apart can be directly compared? He might just as well have gone back to Hereward the Wake.

To me, and I was once a statistician, that single remark removes at a stroke all Brown's credibility on statistics – and what else is there to him other than statistics?

Certainly not counting – or memorizing:

> Indeed, in the pre-Budget report, I told the House that Britain was enjoying the longest period of sustained economic growth for more than 100 years. I have to apologise to the House. Having asked the Treasury to investigate in greater historical detail, I can now report that Britain is enjoying its longest period of sustained economic growth for more than 200 years – the longest period of sustained growth since the beginning of the industrial revolution.
>
> *(Gordon Brown, House of Commons, 17 March 2004)*

A hundred, or two, or three; who cares?

Flash Gordo is not averse to Newspeak either, taking the credit for granting 'independence' to the Bank of England (nationalized in 1946). Yet he selects or nominates the external directors and seven of the nine people making interest rate decisions, which is what 'independence' was all about.

What would Disraeli have made of another 1940s nationalization, the NHS, and its dependence on phoney statistics to survive? (As I argue in Chapter 8, such an animal can never allocate resources in a remotely sensible way. It *has to be* bureaucratic.)

Not a lot, I fancy. The Labour Manifesto sets the scene:

> No one waiting more than 18 weeks from referral to treatment. No
> hidden waits. Free choice of hospital.
>
> *(Labour Party Election Manifesto 2005)*

Shades of the Newspeak shift from 'waiting list' to 'queue' in
Chapter 1.

Now we learn from the *Guardian* on 13 July 2006 that even if
appointment targets of 13 weeks are met, many people have to wait
months more for tests and another six months for treatment. A letter
to the *Sunday Telegraph* provides a typical example:

> My father, aged 84, put his back out in April last year [2005]. He
> waited five months to see a specialist. He then had a scan in Sep-
> tember this year and has just heard that the appointment to hear
> the results of that scan is next February. No one has mentioned the
> possibility of treatment so he continues to manage his pain as best
> he can with over-the-counter analgesics.
>
> *(Letter to the* Sunday Telegraph, *3 December 2006)*

And only a page away in the manifesto is this:

> Survival rates for the biggest killers are improving.
>
> *(Labour Party Election Manifesto 2005)*

Does this count MRSA, including the quadrupling of MRSA deaths
in ten years to 1,600 a year (out of about 18,000 catching the disease
in NHS hospitals)? Or Clostridium Difficile which contributes to
even more deaths than MRSA? On top of that, according to a report
in April 2006 by the National Patient Safety Agency, some 5,000
elderly people die each year due to lack of intensive care, and no fewer
than a whopping 165,000 suffer harm at the hands of the NHS.

The Times of 25 July 2006 cites a report from the Healthcare
Commission which found in a particular hospital (NHS of course) a
disregard for basic hygiene (faeces on bed-rails etc.). 'Hygiene advice
from staff was ignored in favour of government targets', resulting in
the deaths of 65 patients.

Of course there's no holding Patricia (Blew-it) Hewitt. In the springtime her excuse is winter.

> Interviewed on Radio Five Live by Peter Allen about the NHS Hewitt
> said 'we have just come through the coldest winter for 40 years'.
> *(Patricia Hewitt, reported in the* Daily Telegraph, *24 April 2006)*

But a day earlier a *Telegraph* weather correspondent says that in fact while it was the coldest for 9 years in the southern quarter of the UK (although the mean temperature was close to long term average) it was warmer than average in central and northern areas and the warmest for 14 years in Scotland (Philip Eden, *Sunday Telegraph*, 23 April 2006).

On 26 April, on what became Black Wednesday for the Labour Party, Hewitt blew it again, saying that the NHS had just had its 'best year ever', only to be booed by nurses.

After that it was downhill all the way – in August she gave her blessing to *minimum* waiting times – yes, minimum, while the Department of Health admitted that about 20 per cent of ambulance trusts misreported their response times (in which direction – don't ask). The next month she called for 'heat maps' linking potential hospital closures to non-Labour constituencies. This is the lady who wrote a book called *The Abuse of Power*. It takes one to know one.

Finally, though, the truth began to penetrate. In a speech to the Institute for Public Policy Research on 19 September she blurted out:

> [The NHS] no longer knows where it is going. Where will we be in
> five years, ten years, fifteen years time?
>   For all the extra money, all the extra staff and extra patients
> treated, NHS production has remained almost unmoved.
> *(Patricia Hewitt, speech to IPPR, 19 September 2006)*

And after the binge on salaries, Patsy, the number of scanners (per head) is one of the lowest in the civilized world. Fancy that.

Trouble was, she forgot to tell her boss:

> My Honourable Friend is right to say that there has been enormous
> progress in the health service. Waiting lists are down by some

400,000. The number of deaths from heart disease has fallen since
1997 by about 150,000. We now have no one waiting for more than
six months; when we took office, thousands were waiting more
than 18 months. There have been improvements in cancer care,
treatment for cataracts, and in accident and emergency services.

(Tony Blair, House of Commons, 11 October 2006)

So much for the NFS (National Funeral Service).

Disraeli would surely be no happier with the NDS (National Dis-education Service):

1997:   42nd in the World Education League.
2005:   Third best in the world for literacy at age ten and fastest
          improving for maths.

(Labour Party Election Manifesto 2005)

Selective or what? Where were we in the World Education League in
2005, and what was our age ten ranking in 1997?

At least that one was a blatant con-trick. Higher Education
Minister Bill Rammell prefers downright untruths:

The figures he brandished, he said, showed that higher-achieving
schools overpredicted on behalf of their pupils, easing their way to
the elite university of their choice by attracting generous condi-
tional offers. More cautious schools with a poor academic track
record, meanwhile, tended to underpredict. It made an alluring
theory. *And it was flat-out wrong.* [My italics] As we report today,
the figures in front of Mr Rammell showed precisely the opposite. It
is underachieving schools that tend to exaggerate on behalf of
their pupils, while the independent sector tends to underpredict.

(Bill Rammell, as reported in The Times, *8 October 2005)*

For which he is rewarded with an inflationary title 'Minister for Education and Lifelong Learning'. Makes you yearn for John Major's
'University of Life'.

The statistics of his new boss are equally appalling:

Mr. Johnson will today tell the UK Youth Parliament meeting at Leicester University that young people must be praised for excelling in exams. 'We should be celebrating the fact that pass rates are going up and attainment is rising,' he will say. 'Despite the received wisdom of those that seek to detract from the achievements of our young people, research shows young people's performance is improving.'

(Alan Johnson, reported in The Times, *24 July 2006)*

If he gets booed he can call up the heavies:

We have come an immense way in the past eight years, and there is no doubt about the improvement in schools – in particular, the number of failing schools has been more than halved in the past few years. However, Labour Members will not rest while children still do not get the education that they need, which is why the programme of improvement through investment and reform will continue.

(Tony Blair, House of Commons, 8 February 2006)

Ruth Kelly next:

I am glad the Hon. Gentleman welcomes our commitment to diversity in the school system, which has driven up standards in every school across the country over the past eight years.

(Ruth Kelly, House of Commons, 9 February 2006)

It's hard to find any non-politico who doesn't say exactly the opposite. *The Business* is especially outspoken:

For all its intellectual snobbery, Great Britain is one of the worst-educated countries in the developed world. One in six lacks the literacy skills of an 11-year-old, one in three has no basic school-leaving qualifications – twice the level of France or Germany. So it is quite right that on Monday Gordon Brown, Britain's Prime-Minister-in-waiting, will be launching an 'education for all' campaign. The problem is that he is doing so in Mozambique.

*(*The Business, *9 April 2006)*

Whom do you believe? Here's a hint: primary school results are usually published before GCSE results but in 2006 the truly awful primary results were published *together with* GCSE results; this led to a call from the Statistics Commission for an explanation – the correct one being of course that an attempt was made to 'bury' the bad news. Nationalized compulsory education is all rather strange when you consider that it began because of the myth that voluntary education wasn't available to (or was unattractive to) the poor. But I suppose the excuse is that after half a century of the Farewell State, the poor are still growing in number. Using figures from the Department of Work and Pensions (which would want to see lower rather than higher numbers) David Green of Civitas has calculated that one in three households receive more than half their income from the state – up from one in twenty in the 1960s. The law of unintended rewards is at work: any transfer of welfare increases the value of being a recipient.

The 'War on Poverty', like all government 'Wars', continues, with the Welfare State turning temporary misfortunes into career choices – for both recipients and social workers. Hilary Armstrong, Minister for Social Exclusion (the emphasis on 'for', with particular reference to divorced fathers!) tells us that:

> In the last nine years this Labour Government has turned the tide of unemployment, under-investment in public services and the social collapse that threatened to drown our nation in the 1980s . . .
>
> We have had nine consecutive years of investment and reform, with rising incomes for 95 per cent of the population.
>
> *(Hilary Armstrong, Labour Party Conference 2006)*

That unemployment tide will be based on the Newspeak definition in Chapter 1, of course. And it'll exclude all those on benefits, no doubt.

But I digress. Are you thinking what I'm thinking? What's coming next?

Ah, here it is:

> But this broad success has meant we see more clearly the poorest two and a half per cent that have become even more separated because the people above them have improved their lives . . .
>
> The Labour Party is proud of creating universal public services

because they are for everyone, but sometimes a one-size-fits-all
approach lets down our most needy and hard-to-reach.

(Hilary Armstrong, Labour Party Conference 2006)

Do we really see two and a half per cent? What does it mean? Be it two
and a half or twenty-two and a half you have failed, Hilary. No government can help everybody – you'd collect from everybody and give
it back after (a) creating a black hole and (b) taking your cut out of
the rent, so are you inching towards the idea that the Universal
Welfare State was wrong? Has it created the Farewell State instead?

It may interest you to know, silly Hilly, that in the late nineteenth
century, the average middle-class household contributed ten per cent
of its income to charities, whilst half of the artisans and working
classes were weekly subscribers.[2] Most of these charities were aimed at
helping the poor including your 'most needy and hard to reach'. And
the general idea was to reform behaviour and get 'em off benefits asap,
which must seem quaint to your career social workers.

Oh dear. Another U-turn called for? No fear. The Farewell State is
here to stay. The haves, the have nots, the rich, the poor (in both cases
deserving or otherwise) and the never-ending Stalinist social engineering for we're not quite sure what – except more Stalins of course!

Can we see clearly the rich? Who are they? As we asked in Chapter
1, have they high earnings or high assets or both? Doesn't matter, we
hate 'em all. In 1975, the infamous 'Social Contract' told us that
'one-tenth of British adults own between them three quarters of the
nation's private wealth'. My comment concluded that 'it is not difficult to juggle with these figures, adjusting in what seems to be a
reasonable manner for some of these factors,[3] so as to conclude that
the richest 10 per cent of us, far from owning three quarters of the
wealth, own only 15 or 20 per cent of it'.

On top of all that, people in the groups (richest fifth, second richest
. . . poorest fifth etc.) are restless; they just won't keep still – always
moving up or down or across. Most inconsiderate.

---

2 *The Corrosion of Charity*, Robert Whelan, Institute of Economic Affairs, 1996.
3 Unsuitable Estate Duty data, exclusion of certain types of wealth, exclusion of
swathes of people, all family except breadwinners treated as penniless, exclusion of
public wealth, no allowance for wealth increasing with age or for voluntary savings.

And I'm still scratching my head over our old friend Sarah Teather, up there with the best of the illiberals:

> We live in a wealthy country but the riches of prosperity and hope are not open to all. Over 11 million people still live in poverty, and if you are born into a poor family in this country you will probably die in one.
>
> *(Sarah Teather, LibDems Party Conference 2006)*

Like Alan Sugar (born in a council flat), Philip Green (left your beloved education system at 15) and thousands if not millions more. What we can say with confidence is that in a free market (granted, we don't have one) profits and the incomes provided by them are certificates of performance; the higher they are, the greater are the benefits bestowed on others via voluntary transactions. (This claim evolves naturally from the appendix to Chapter 8.)

What we can also say with confidence is that both poor and rich – whether in income or assets – pay high taxes:

> Taxes are already too high. The poorest fifth of households pay £250,000 in tax over a lifetime, a grotesque sum for them. The middle fifth pay more than £500,000; the top fifth pay £1.2 million. The top fifth undoubtedly includes some very rich people, but the majority of taxpayers, even in this group, are not rich at all. Tax falls very heavily on the poor, the old and the middle class. A Conservative Party ought always to be fighting to get tax rates down. There is a strong social case for a low-tax policy.
>
> *(William Rees Mogg,* The Times, *2 October 2006)*

A study by Charlie Elphick for the Centre for Policy Studies using the Office for National Statistics as the sole source of data, concludes that the poorest households in Britain are paying a higher share of tax and getting a lower share of benefits than before Labour came to power, the impact of the Government's policies resembling the Sheriff of Nottingham rather than Robin Hood.

And in the US the top ten per cent of taxpayers pay two-thirds of all income tax and half of all Federal taxes.

How many more numbers do we want? And why?

You can make crime statistics what you want as well. What does the Labour Party want? Some low numbers:

> Today, there is less chance of being a victim of crime than for more than 20 years . . .
>
> *(Labour Party Election Manifesto 2005)*

Yeah, right. Here's a better one:

> The annual crime figures show a surge in street robberies to nearly 100,000 a year.
>
> *(Guardian, 20 July 2006)*

And like NHS waiting lists disappearing into queues, violent crime disappears into cautions (apparently about half of violent crimes vanish in this way – which also means no other punishment).

The Statistics Commission has said that Home Office Ministers should be stripped of their involvement in publishing crime statistics. I would go further and strip *all* ministers from *any* involvement in *any* statistics. (I'd strip them from involvement in anything at all but that's for another day!)

It's not just old cynical me. On 19 November 2006 the *Sunday Telegraph* reported that the Royal Statistical Society said it was 'very anxious' that measures unveiled in the Queen's speech last week, designed to strengthen the Office of National Statistics (ONS), 'do not go far enough'. The Statistics Commission said the Treasury-backed proposals 'skirted around the key issues' – adding that government statisticians 'need protection from abuse by ministers and special advisers'.

The Labour Party's 2005 Manifesto says:

> We fulfilled the promises of our 1997 and 2001 Manifestos. Here is what changed:
>
> *(Labour Party Election Manifesto 2005)*

The list that follows ('prosperity for all, world-class public services, a modern welfare state, strong and safe communities' and so on) is unadulterated statistical crap. If you want a blow-by-blow account read Karyn Miller in the *Sunday Telegraph* of 19 November 2006. Here is a snippet from the section on crime:

May 1997: 'It is intolerable that many of our elderly citizens live in fear of persistent juvenile offenders running riot. In this Queen's Speech, we take the action to put a stop to it.'

September 2006: 'It is simply not acceptable for young children to be left without supervision, parental or otherwise, free to truant, vandalise and roam the streets at all hours. And it is morally wrong for us to stand aside and to be indifferent to it.'

The lesson is that we can't trust politicians with statistics, be they on the topics covered here or any others – economics, health, education, poverty, crime, science, climate, war: you call it, they'll distort it.

Political statistical crap even contaminates the contaminators – all over Europe. Let's sign off with passive smoking:

Passive smoking is killing around 20,000 EU citizens every year, according to new findings unveiled in the European Parliament.

(From eupolitix.com, 21 March 2006)

The UK agrees; according to Magnus Linklater in *The Times* of 22 March 2006, the UK evidence comes from the Government's Scientific Committee on Tobacco and Health, which says that the evidence for damage caused by second-hand smoking is 'conclusive'.

Yet Professor Richard Doll, the first scientist to publish research suggesting a link between smoking and lung cancer, said on Radio 4 in 2001 that 'the effect of other people smoking in my presence is so small that it doesn't worry me'.

Whatever their stripes, all politicos play the statistics game for all they are worth. And if there aren't any they can use the 'precautionary principle' to justify finding some.

Here is *The Times* lauding higher taxes for research – for its own sake:

Dozens of scientists and much of the mobile phone industry may wonder why Professor Lawrie Challis is planning an expensive study of 200,000 mobile users to establish as definitively as possible whether handsets pose an increased risk of cancer . . .

This is not because there is any compelling evidence of a link between mobile phone use and serious disease. On the contrary, there is no such evidence – yet . . .

The precautionary principle still applies here. Manufacturers as well as users should welcome the new study.

(Leading article, The Times, *20 January 2007)*

But not non-users, or small-time users, who just have to stump up. Why not study the nature of the toxic qualities that lead to politics as a career? Sweaty feet or sticky fingers? Or discover why brown cows give white milk when they only eat green grass? Could lead to a non-green revolution. The much used excuse, the precautionary principle, is a sham. Endless testing of new drugs by the state kills people who are waiting. The costs and benefits of research can never be determined in advance – except that if it's taxpayer-funded, we can bet that even the most rudimentary statistics will disclose awful success rates.

I wonder what Disraeli said about the statistics leading to the Forster Act of 1870, by which school education was made compulsory and eventually nationalized. Forster relied on evidence from a 'dodgy dossier' in the shape of a very small survey in 1869, ignoring the much more comprehensive Newcastle Commission evidence. This latter showed that over 95 per cent of children attended school regularly for several years (probably better than today, with a literacy rate that was *certainly* better) – and that parents were the largest contributors to school fees.

At least Disraeli's time, buttressed by free trade and free movement across most of Europe, was one of peace. Not so the twentieth century and so far the twenty-first. Another dodgy tax-payer funded dossier became the excuse for the invasion of Iraq, now revealed as one of the most unprincipled decisions ever, with an aftermath of murder and chaos on a massive scale, all too predictable yet supported or condoned by all three major parties.

Time to start another chapter.

5

Cheeky Crap

The weaker the argument, the stronger the words.

(Anon)

My introductory remarks to the first edition (1975) seem to have stood the test of time, along with the cheek, so here they are again.

Sometimes, if you haven't got a leg to stand on, it's amazing how far you can get by being bold and vociferous. Through sheer audacity you can *make* someone believe you if you speak loudly and sound cocksure enough. Occasionally it backfires and the listener thinks 'By gum, he's got a nerve', but other times it works like a dream. In fact I fancy they're getting away with most of it. Certainly if they're not it's not for lack of trying, as this chapter makes clear.

Actually I've been a bit cheeky myself and tarted the above up a bit. All it's really saying is that if you've got no case (as is likely for politicians) then attack is the best form of defence.

Staying with the first edition for a moment, the Labour Party was still on the nationalization kick:

The Labour Government will take into public ownership land required for development, redevelopment and improvement. These proposals do not apply to owner-occupiers, whose homes and gardens will be safeguarded.

(Labour Party Election Manifesto October 1974)

What could I say but 'Gee thanks. Jolly sporting of you'.

Nowadays we hear few cries for outright nationalization, and the reason is simple; the Tories spotted it at the time:

Nationalisation is inefficient, hugely expensive and totally unneces-
sary. The desired results can be achieved just as effectively and far
more cheaply through taxation and regulation.

(Conservative Party Election Manifesto October 1974)

Fascism, it's called: we own, they control – even our homes and
gardens. Home Information Packs, draconian Empty Dwelling Management Orders on inherited property, punitive taxes on second
homes, hosepipe bans (on all except 'ASBO' Blair).

The floodgates of the Tories' discovery, state regulation (i.e. corporatism), are wide open – a new regulation about every quarter of an
hour, day and night throughout the year. Those nasty things called
businesses which the politicians tell you are out to screw you (by competing with each other for your voluntary custom – yes it's crap of
course) are easy targets:

Passengers are being 'held to ransom' by train operators who have
proved incapable of offering reasonable fares, an all-party committee of MPs said yesterday.

(David Millward, Daily Telegraph, 20 May 2006)

For 'train operators' read 'Alistair Darling' (see Chapter 2).

The Government must now pick up the pieces and set about
creating a coherent policy for the railways which also incorporates
better regulation of fares and conditions of travel.

(David Millward, Daily Telegraph, 20 May 2006)

Et tu, David.

The other David (Cameron – a corporatist if ever there was one)
had attacked BHS for selling sexy underwear for children; the range
had actually been withdrawn three years earlier. No mention of Philip
Green as an entrepreneurial role model.

In the same speech (see below) our Dave gave us a straw man: 'If a
supermarket drives down prices to force small shops out of business
and then immediately puts prices up again – we need to complain'.
That won't take long, Dave, because it's never happened.

But his real cheek in this odyssey was this:

> We should never subcontract to the Government the job of making
> our country a better place to live in.
>
> *(David Cameron, speech to Business in the Community, 9 May 2006)*

The current costs of (enforced) subcontracting are half of the national
income.[1] Can we have just *some* of it back? No:

> I'd like us to think not about how we give people a tax cut but how
> we give them a time increase.
>
> *(David Cameron reported in* The Times, *21 July 2006)*

Forget that we could give ourselves a time increase if he hadn't swiped
50 per cent of our money! The saddest part is that his starting point
(in line with all politicos) is that Government owns everything and we
have to plead for crumbs.

Not surprising then that British business is 'facing a billion pound
assault by consumer groups as ministers prepare to allow a version of
US-style class actions against dodgy retailers and shoddy workmanship' (reported in *The Times* of 17 July 2006). We can guess who the
'consumer groups' will be – yes, the powers will be given to 'public
bodies, such as council-run trading standards departments'.

Government expands by any way it can. Regulations proliferate,
and tax proliferates too. (If we want to be fussy, so does nationalization – *we* have been nationalized for six months out of twelve.)

How's this for cheek:

> They [the Labour Government] even think they can spend our
> money better than we can.
>
> *(David Davis, Conservative Party Conference 2006)*

But you shared the platform with your boss, who has vowed on
numerous occasions not to reduce tax – 'until it can be afforded'. I've
a better idea – we'll defer our tax payments until they can be afforded.

There's no way the Lib Dems will be any better either:

---

1 A better measure than GDP; the latter ignores depreciation.

> The people of this country have an outstanding record of helping those in need around the world. It is time for our government to match their commitment.
>
> *(Liberal Democrats Election Manifesto 2005)*

And our *government's* money comes from? Cut out the middle man, I say.

In the utterly bizarre world of politics – the real area of dodgy selling and shoddy workmanship – Gordo has to tell us that his hyper-spend on the NHS has shown results:

> Let us remind the country that the NHS is our greatest achievement and I am proud that free at the point of use we can aspire to it being for all people the best and fairest insurance policy in the world.
>
> *(Gordon Brown, Labour Party Conference 2006)*

Glad you said, 'Aspire to it', Gordo. We've been 'aspiring', perspiring even, for over 50 years while we've watched it slide down to one of the worst insurance policies in Europe.

Perhaps Gordon ('only the State can guarantee fairness'[2]) Brown was also responsible for this snorter:

> We will promote the integration of health and social care at local level, so that older people and those with long-term conditions can retain their independence.
>
> *(Labour Party Election Manifesto 2005)*

Oh yes? Here's some real dodgy selling – mis-selling in its full glory:

> The Commission for Social Care Inspection reports today that nearly two thirds of the 150 councils that provide social services changed their criteria last year to provide social care only for the *most dependent* people [my italics].
>
> *(Jill Sherman, The Times, 30 November 2006)*

---

2 Speech to the Centre for (wait for it!) Social Justice, 18 January 2006.

Tony Blair can hide shoddy workmanship with a slippery tongue:

> I have spoken to NHS staff in Coventry, Edinburgh and Swansea,
> who tell me how their new hospital and the new funding is letting
> them improve care for their patients.
>
> *(Tony Blair, Labour Party Election Manifesto 2005)*

Funny then, Tone, that according to a survey by the Healthcare Commission only a third of hospital staff would be happy to be treated in
their own hospital.

Sometimes a watchdog has teeth:

> Patient choice is damaging hospitals, says NHS watchdog.
>
> *(Jill Sherman,* The Times, *11 October 2005)*

That says it all. And so does Patsy:

> We have written a very big cheque for the NHS, but it is not a blank
> cheque. Money that is wasted or spent inefficiently means less for
> patients who need treatment.
>
> *(Patricia Hewitt, 25 January 2006, as reported in* The Times, *11 March 2006)*

At the same time *The Times* of 11 March 2006 revealed that our Pat
had hired a speech-writer at a cost of £70 an hour. That'll be the blank
cheque then.

Let's leave the NIS (National Infection Service) for the NDS
(National Diseducation Service), because I think I can see something
sensible from Labour:

> We must combine the broadest base of participation with the
> ability for the most talented to progress to the very top.
>
> *(Labour Party Election Manifesto 2005)*

Shomething wrong shomewhere, shurely. Yes – I spoke too soon. I
thought it was about academic excellence. But I've just realized it was
about sport. We can't encourage *academic* excellence, now can we?

Flash Gordon has flashy ideas. In his March 2006 Budget he
announced a long term 'aspiration' ('ere we go) to lift spending on
state schools from £5,500 per pupil to the *current* figure, £8,000, for
independent schools (forgetting to mention that as much as half of

his £5,500 is eaten up by intervening agencies). In September he announced it again – as *another* new initiative. All in a day's work.

Of course an aspiration is not a promise. We must hope not, or we'll find that the money's been spent on spreading the new religion of man-made global warming, brooking no dissent. As this book becomes complete in February 2007, Alan Johnson is pushing the Qualifications and Curriculum Authority – yes, Stalinist isn't it? – hard on this very point. In the next chapter I show that about the only truth in the 'global warming' controversy is that there is indeed raging controversy. As usual, the latest report from the IPCC, the UN's Intergovernmental Panel on Climate Change, has a 'Summary for Policy-Makers' (i.e. politicos) which bears little relation to the main report. (This doctoring is one of the many examples of the politicization of science referred to in Chapter 6.) And in the meantime new theories sprout up all the time, including the recent idea that global warming is due to fluctuations in cosmic rays.

Except amongst the politicians, including the Lib Dems:

Conference, the scientific evidence is clear: global warming is a man-made problem . . .

(Chris Huhne, Liberal Democrats Party Conference 2006)

What is clear, Mr Hoon (whoops, sorry, Huhne, but does it really matter?) is that the scientific evidence is NOT clear. You must know this as well as I do. But politicians depend on statistical crap to make their case for controlling us – your subjects. The politics of fear, it's called. And so you quote the numbers you want – almost invariably from Government (or worse, UN) sources which are often corrupt and sometimes *deliberately* misused (see Chapter 7), to scare us.

There is a great deal of similarity in the way the politicians treat environmentalism, war and terror, the underlying tactic being to create fear and dependence. We all know about 'the war on terror', 'the war on poverty', 'the war on drugs' and so on, and 'the war on warming' is on the way. The environmentalist movement has plenty of links with fascism and plenty of eco-warriors who don't really care for human beings.[3]

The First World War had its roots in anti-trade; the next could come via carbon emissions. Big Government, 'democratic' or otherwise, will soon forget the lessons of Iraq, namely that as Martin Samuels says in *The Times* of 14 November 2006, 'One of the main reasons to oppose the invasion of Iraq was its entirely predictable aftermath.' In turn, and in brief, this aftermath has left Iraq in a far sorrier plight than ever and both the UK and the USA are much more dangerous places as a result.

The Labour Party has never learned the lesson of Iraq – or hadn't in time for its Manifesto in April 2005:

> It is right that we do everything in our power to disrupt terrorist networks, and to challenge the conditions that help to breed terrorism.
>
> *(Labour Party Election Manifesto 2005)*

Like invading Iraq (under a dodgy dossier to boot), and bombing it for about a dozen years beforehand? And like invading *our* liberties in a fruitless attempt to deal with the additional terrorists you created? By the time November 2006 came round you were forced to admit, grudgingly, that the invasion was a mistake. Thanks mate.

Over the pond in Big Government USA, George Bush is his usual masterful self – and economical with the truth, not to put too fine a point on it:

> Fellow citizens, we've been called to leadership in a period of consequence. We've entered a great ideological conflict we did nothing to invite.
>
> *(George W Bush, State of the Union Address, 31 January 2006)*

---

3 See The Dark Side of Environmentalism at *MineYourOwnbusiness.org*

Except bombing and sanctions over most of the 1990s, killing hundreds of thousands if not millions of innocent civilian Iraqis, lots of them children. Or are you saying that was mostly those nasty Democrats (true) and you, of course, wouldn't have behaved like that?

The *New York Times* is in big trouble for doing its job. Now we're into seriously dangerous cheek:

> George Bush and Dick Cheney are calling *The New York Times* a disgrace, Republican congressmen say it is guilty of treason and demand the prosecution of the Editor, while a right-wing radio presenter suggests most of its readers must be 'jihadists' . . .
>
> The newspaper's offence was to publish an article revealing that the US Administration had kept tabs on suspected terrorists by tapping into bank records which track global transactions.
>
> *(Reported in* The Times, *29 June 2006)*

An offence which some members of congress and prominent media commentators call 'treason' and suggest an 'Office of Censorship'.

And while we're at it, we've been keeping tabs on the lot of you anyway:

> In the wake of the May 11 revelation by USA Today of a massive telephone spying program by the National Security Agency, directed against nearly every American citizen, the media commentary has deliberately downplayed the sinister nature of the program.
>
> This is a deliberate cover-up of what is without question the most wide-ranging invasion of privacy by the federal government in US history.
>
> *(Patrick Martin, edstrong.blog-city.com, 16 May 2006)*

All under cover of the misnamed Patriot Act, which concentrates on American citizens and abolishes habeas corpus.

And it's hard to see how getting involved in every complex conflict around the globe enhances national security. And American soldiers are in plenty of other countries too – over 150 of them, including the UK, Germany, Italy and Japan.

Anyway, if you step out of line in the land of the free they bang you up. The USA has by far the largest number of prisoners in the world, relative to its population. (It'll have more soon; the Democratic Party Platform of 2004 pledges to 'crack down on gang violence and drug crime'.)

And the UK has the biggest percentage in the EU. In a speech on 10 May 2006 in Oxford, the Lord Chief Justice, Lord Phillips of Worth Matravers, talked of the alternatives to custody – and was slapped down in no uncertain terms by John Reid, just five days into his new job of Home Secretary.

Jack Straw, a former Home Secretary, backed up Reid:

> I wish it were possible to deal with criminals outside prison but most people who end up in prison go there because community punishments have failed.
>
> *(Jack Straw reported in* The Times, *19 June 2006)*

But 'community punishments' are not the only alternatives are they Jack? Anyone ever told you about the criminal compensating the victim – with hard cash? And how about a bit of *DE*-criminalizing – or RE-legalizing, certainly a better description with regard to drug offences. That'd let out 20 per cent of 'criminals' at a stroke. They've already done that in Portugal – and Mexico. And it would do wonders in the USA too – a 50 per cent reduction! Wonders also for the price of drugs and therefore the genuine crimes of theft committed to be able to afford drugs. A virtuous circle instead of a vicious one. We all win – except organized crime – which *includes terrorism*. The illegality and the consequential high price of drugs plays no small part in financing terrorism. Politicos everywhere, put that in your pipe of peace and smoke it.

Unfortunately, the politicos have more important fish to fry, usually to strengthen their own positions. Take Jack Straw for example, the driving force behind an attempt to keep Lord Phillips and all those other Lords well out of the way, or make 'em all men of Straw.

> Ministers are to consult Labour MPs on a system of indirect elections to the House of Lords to prevent the reformed second chamber from rivalling the Commons.
>
> *(Reported in* The Times, *26 August 2006)*

The *Times* Leader had it right: A House of Lackeys.

Strange that Straw should be trying to change things anyway:

> We are on any measure one of the most successful peacetime governments of the past 100 years.
>
> *(Jack Straw, Labour Party Conference 2006)*

Whoa there. Steady on, Jack. How about the quality of the Deputy Prime Minister, John Prescott, who made such a wonderful speech at your *1996* conference?

> Can you believe that this lot is in charge? Not for long, eh? Then after 17 years of this Tory government, they have the audacity to talk about morality. Did you hear John Major on the *Today* programme? – calling for ethics to come back into the political debate? I'm told some Tory MPs think ethics is a county near Middlesex. It's a bit hard to take: John Major – ethics man . . . For too many Tories, morality means not getting caught. Morality is measured in more than money. It's about right and wrong. We are a party of principle. We will earn the trust of the British people. We've had enough lies. Enough sleaze.
>
> *(John Prescott, Labour Party Conference 1996)*

You'd think that after all that has happened since, including a bit of non-monetary stuff on the side, a seasoned journo like Peter Riddell wouldn't jump to defend him over the scandal about his attempt to fast-track the Millennium Dome into a casino:

> I do not believe that Mr Prescott behaved corruptly; he does not have a role in decisions about who runs casinos. Moreover, his failure to log the visit in the Register of Members' Interests was a mistake, as he implicitly recognised yesterday in making a belated declaration. But it was not of itself an outrage.
>
> *(Peter Riddell, The Times, 6 July 2006)*

Well, Peter, you didn't behave corruptly either, but you certainly got your facts wrong. The inevitable happened in November:

So it comes as no surprise to learn, as we did this week, that, despite all those protestations to the contrary, John Prescott had indeed been party to discussions between government officials and Philip Anschutz about the prospects for a super casino being built at the Dome. The admission, when it came, was without contrition. This Government does not do shame. That was apparent from its early days, when the arrival of Bernie Ecclestone's cheque coincided with a convenient change of heart on tobacco advertising.

(Patience Wheatcroft, Sunday Telegraph, *12 November 2006)*

Prescott must be well up the list in the Rewards for Failure syndrome that pervades a government which dares to talk of 'shoddy workmanship' in the private sector.

Ken Livingstone can't be far behind:

> The London mayor, Ken Livingstone, today received beefed-up powers as a reward for delivering 'strong leadership' over the past six years, Ruth Kelly, the Secretary of State for Communities and Local Government, said.
>
> The government made good its manifesto pledge by introducing major changes for the Greater London Authority, including wider mayoral powers over housing, skills, planning and the environment.
>
> Ms Kelly said that the London government had enhanced democracy and provided strong leadership for the capital.
>
> *(Reported in* Guardian Unlimited, *13 July 2006)*

Livingstone is the buffoon who was elected by 16 per cent of the London electorate and who has lorded it ever since. Calling the US Ambassador 'a chiselling little crook' for the Embassy's decision that its diplomats shouldn't pay Ken's congestion charge (do *you* pay, Ken?) is entirely typical. And as Martin Samuel says in *The Times* of 11 April 2006, 'he will follow the money, just like Mr Prescott, just like Tony Blair, just like grasping politicians who see no brutality and corruption in modern China, but cash and contracts'.

Hazel Blears sees the god of 'democracy' as an end in itself, not a means of preserving liberty. It doesn't matter a jot whether it produces a Hitler or a Jefferson. So her speech about 'The Democratic Demographic Time Bomb' came as she saw approval of Big Government dwindling into apathy. Jolly good thing I say, and you can stuff your 'Citizenship' – now a compulsory school subject.

Why does she think democracy is so good?

> Because without democracy, there is only tyranny or dictatorship.
> *(Hazel Blears speech, 7 November 2006)*

And *with* it, Hazel, there is also tyranny and dictatorship (not all the time, but sometimes, irrespective of 'Democracy'). And there I'm being generous; majority rule is still *rule*, which is hardly a natural bedfellow of freedom. Democracy gets no mention at all in the US Declaration of Independence, the Constitution, or the Bill of Rights – the founders knew that freedom is chipped away in every democracy there has ever been, until the structure breaks.

But meanwhile it's great for the rulers, eh Hazel? As a letter to *The Times* on 23 September 2006 noted, 'Hazel Blears wants the taxpayer to plug the gap in the Labour Party's finances. Does this mean that every taxpayer will receive a peerage?' Not only that. She wants more 'plugging' than other parties 'as the party of government'.

How about us paying according to how *much* you repeal and how *little* you add? As Jamie Whyte says in a *Times* article on 13 November 2006 ('Why voting is a waste of time'): 'When you can ballot with your wallet, who needs a pencil and a piece of string?' He might have added 'in order to empower the politicians to take half of your wallet away and to tell you what you can and can't do with the other half'.

There are two kinds of Democracy: the Political kind and the Market kind. Is that in your National Curriculum? Love to have your take, Haze, on the political democracies of Hitler, Mussolini, Putin, and of course the European Union – that group of politicians whose accounts haven't been signed off for well over a decade? The lot who wrote a constitution which has been rejected by the people of every government that dared to put it to a vote, but who carry on regardless? The lot whose Common Agricultural Policy takes up half the lolly and redistributes it mainly from poor to rich in what amounts to a welfare state in reverse?

Here's the boss:

Last week, to celebrate Europe Day, and with an eye to the approaching 50th anniversary of the Treaty of Rome next year, it was the turn of Jose-Manuel Barroso, the little Portuguese apparatchik who is President of the European Commission.

Publishing a 'Citizens' Agenda for Europe', he declared that what we citizens want is 'more Europe'.

(Reported in Christopher Booker's Notebook,
Sunday Telegraph, *14 May 2006)*

Good word that, apparatchik. Lots of democracies have them, Hazel, as they have records of belligerence and war rather than peace.[4]

I can't let this chapter close before another quick look at Europe's top apparatchik, cheek personified:

Britain is preparing to give up the national veto on EU law-and-order legislation after Brussels demanded that national governments surrender control of key policies to combat terrorism and organised crime . . .

Senhor Barroso said that he would ask heads of government to 'transfer to the Community a large number of the decisions in the fields of justice, freedom and security that can be dealt with more effectively at European level than at national level' . . .

'The most effective response in the field of security is the European response,' he said. 'People are asking for "more Europe" in order to combat terrorism and organised crime. It is our duty to respond to this appeal, with or without a constitution.'

(Jose-Manuel Barroso, reported in The Times, *9 June 2006)*

Which people would these be, Senhor? Your reference to the constitution comes because this proposal was in the draft European Constitution – resoundingly rejected by voters wherever they were asked.

Beat that, Hazel.

Oh I forgot; the Senhor's term of office is over. Another apparatchik? You decide:

---

4 See for example, Robert Skidelsky's article in *The Times* of 17 September 2005 ('A fatal flaw at the heart of Bush and Blair's democratic crusade').

Vanhanen [the new President] continued: 'The Union's weakening legitimacy is due in part to the fact that citizens do not know what the Union does for them. Many of the things . . . such as the right to live, work and study anywhere in the Union – are taken for granted. People forget that such things are possible only because of the Union.'

(Matti Vanhanen, Plenary Session of European Parliament, reported by tcsdaily.com, 15 August 2006)

One hundred years ago, Mr Vanhanen, you were free to go anywhere in Europe whenever you liked. Many people did.

6

Illogical Crap

Contrariwise, continued Tweedledee, if it was so, it might be; and if it were so, it would be: but as it is it ain't. That's logic.

(Lewis Carroll)

So far, I hope that the nature of the crap in each chapter hasn't caused too much head-scratching. I also hope that this and the following chapters have the same feature but for one reason or another, a little more signposting may help. In unfamiliar topics, logic or the lack of it is not always easy to spot.

Three major topics were barely political issues in 1975: the environment, war and terrorism. (Actually the environment *was* an issue in one respect: global cooling!) In fact all three are strongly linked (Margaret Beckett gave us an inkling in Chapter 3) and all three are best resolved *without* government.

Concerns about pollution and the environment are a godsend for government – our fears become their income. This chapter gives them some serious attention (including an Appendix) but it also covers several other issues where logic is prominent via its absence.

In the first edition (1975), the first few pages of this chapter were taken up with energy and the 1974 oil 'crisis', with prices having quadrupled in pretty short order. Doomsayers were legion, including the *Guardian*'s City Editor:

> to go on underlining the probability, some would say the near cer-
> tainty, that within thirty or forty years we shall be coming to the
> end of our oil reserves . . .
>
> Such is the energy jag, compounded by assumptions that the free
> market price will arrive by its own inner wisdom at the greatest
> happiness for the greatest number.
>
> *(Harford Thomas,* Guardian, *24 May 1974)*

After thirty-odd years oil reserves are virtually infinite – at least
75,000 years' worth and still counting.

And why should the 'energy jag' be *compounded* by the free market
price (which, by the way, we haven't seen for at least 100 years). Why
not *resolved*, for instance, which is exactly what free market prices do?

Harford's editorial bosses were no better:

> the cool words of the White Paper should be noted. 'If prices
> remain high and with the high production now expected, profits
> on our offshore oil will be enormous . . .
>
> The result is that North Sea licensees would reap enormous and
> uncovenanted profits on their investment.
>
> *(Guardian leader, 12 July 1974)*

I asked whether it seemed 'cool' that a White Paper is presumptuous
and (as it happened) entirely wrong? (I mean 'cool' as in 'moderate,
calm or measured' not 'hot stuff'.)

Unfortunately it *is* hot stuff in the shape of 'global warming' that no
politico is cool about today. Here's *The Times'* US Editor:

> Therefore, Pascal said, the sensible thing to do is to resist the
> atheist temptation. The best on offer is a lifelong sense of smug
> superiority in this world. The worst is eternal damnation . . .
>
> This is where our friend Pascal comes in. If we believe in global
> warming and do something about it and it turns out we're right,
> then we're, climatologically speaking, redeemed – if not for ever, at
> least until some other threat to our existence comes along.
>
> If we're wrong about it, what is the ultimate cost? A world with
> improved energy efficiency and quite a lot of ugly windmills.
>
> *(Gerard Baker,* The Times, *15 September 2006)*

Now I don't want to get hot under the collar about religion but no atheist should accept the argument to become a Christian, a Buddhist, or anything else 'just in case'; not only is it an uninviting argument but also it begs the question: which one of the many saviours from hell and damnation on offer should you choose?

The global warming argument is just as bad. Redemption will not come for a rich and imperialistic western world that wants to pull up the drawbridge on the rest, dooming all to a much lower living standard – and perhaps another world war – on the basis of a possibility. In my view a remote possibility, but for logic's sake I'm trying to keep cool for now. In any case improved energy efficiency is the very last thing that could come out of lowering CO_2 emissions. See also the Appendix and references at the end of this chapter.

On this topic statists show their colours in every newspaper:

> Stern is wonderfully clear. Assuming the scientific neo-consensus on global warming and its causes to be broadly right, Stern examines the economics of doing a lot to cut emissions versus doing little, and concludes that doing a lot will most likely save us a great deal of money as well as trouble and death . . .
>
> And this is the message we must absorb from Stern – that the only option that should be ruled out is doing nothing.
>
> *(David Aaronovitch,* The Times, *21 October 2006)*

There we go again; *assuming*. There may be a neo-con consensus, David, but there is no scientific consensus – far from it. There is a *political* consensus, alongside much scientific *opposition* (for example, here is an extract from a letter to the *Sunday Telegraph* of 7 May 2006, from Mr Robert Pate; there are many more):

> As for Lord Rees's so-called consensus of scientists, I can produce the names (in alphabetical order) of more than 19,000 scientists who disagree.

Thank goodness Ann Treneman is around. On the same day her Parliamentary Sketch is entitled 'Hot-air production and emissions of gobbledygook reach a new high'.

Far from global warming being 'the greatest market failure ever seen' as Stern and Gordon Brown say, this report is government failure in action. The weekend magazine *The Business* is right on the button on 4 November 2006 – describing the Stern report as 'the ecology equivalent of a Blairite dodgy dossier'. One glaring error amongst many is that Stern, an economist, fails to discount any of the doom-laden numbers to the present day to allow for interest; he treats a pound in 2050 as a pound today instead of less than 25p. Dodgy or what?

Lack of logic on the environment pervades the whole climate – not only global warming but also pollution and conservation. If two little boys each have a glass of lemonade and a straw, how quickly do you think they'll drink it? A lot slower, and a lot more peacefully, than if they have the same amount of lemonade in one glass with two straws. This is Garrett Hardin's 'tragedy of the commons' – private ownership means more conservation and husbandry. Look at private gardens, beaches, parks and rivers versus their 'publicly' owned (i.e. government owned) counterparts. Technically private ownership of seas and airspace is becoming more feasible by the day (governments profess to own airspace and certain sea space already) yet rarely does one read about its benefits to the environment and peace.

Here is an illustration of what we do get, ad nauseam:

> Over-fishing of cod has already led to the collapse of cod fisheries worldwide. Cod was depleted in the Bering Sea in the 1980s and centuries of fishing in the Grand Banks off the coast of Newfoundland ended in the 1990s when Atlantic cod was fished to commercial extinction.
>
> *(Valerie Elliott,* The Times, *21 June 2006)*

Here we have a two-page spread (specially titled 'Conservation') on the issue. No mention of 'the tragedy of the commons' (i.e. of public or government ownership), rivers or lakes, fish farms, and so on. And what on earth (or in water!) does 'commercial extinction' mean?

Private property rights are one of the prerequisites of any civilized society, as well as by far the most effective means of conservation available. But in the world of Big Government and vested interests, we're speeding in the opposite direction: less *private* property and more *public* property to fight over.

Or to leave to rot:

> Less than 2 per cent of tropical coral reefs are properly protected from illegal fishing, mining or pollution despite government promises of wider safeguards, a study published in the journal *Science* showed yesterday.
>
> 'The figures are depressing,' said Camilo Mora, a scientist at Dalhousie University in Canada and lead author of the study, carried out in New Zealand by researchers from seven nations. 'Many countries create marine protected areas and then forget about them,' he said.
>
> *(Reported in* The Times, *23 June 2006)*

Needless to say, the failures are on government property. The study finds that only about ten per cent of 'Marine Protected Areas' have sound management. The recommendation? Sound management, of course! Magic!

As a rule, governments don't do conservation. The real answer is staring them in the face. There are plenty of *private* coral reefs,[1] beautifully cared for. 'Private reefs', you say, 'you're kidding.' No, I'm not. All you need is an old wreck of a bus and somebody to 'drag and drop' it a few miles out. Take your bearings and within weeks a sophisticated community of plants, fish and other marine life will have become established. Catch or use some of it and conserve the rest! And private lakes are a doddle.

And it's not technically difficult to achieve more general private ownership, in Antarctica, oceans, airspace, or other parts of the solar system, thus going a long way to solve pollution problems too.[2] National governments already claim or purloin their own seas for fishing limits, airspace for taxing airlines who cross it, or for selling off frequencies – as if they were theirs in the first place!

---

1 For example, there are private reefs off several US states (including Alabama and Georgia), Japan, Thailand and the UK.

2 On private ownership see Curran Kemp, Mises Institute, 19 December 2006. On pollution, by 1830 both the UK and the USA fully recognized private airspace rights, allowing owners to sue (for example) factory owners for damages from emissions. Over the following century these rights were removed as governments claimed eminent domain – often resulting in more smoke-belching factories!

Heady, unfamiliar stuff for many. Time for calmer waters? OK, we're pretty safe with the National Diseducation Service – although the obvious answer is missed there too:

> Alan Johnson, the Education Secretary, has decided that the new Violent Crime Reduction Bill does not go far enough in tackling the knife culture in schools and wants to give head teachers wider powers to track down and seize knives . . .
>
> The change would mean that many innocent pupils would be caught up in searches. It is certain to be challenged by civil liberties groups.
>
> *(Rosemary Bennett,* The Times, *3 July 2006)*

The only crap here is that these powers need to be legislated in the first place. There is no issue in the independent schools; they simply act as the owners they are. Is it a crime to check whether someone has knife before letting them into your car or your home – or your airport? Would civil liberties groups really challenge that? 'Who owns a State school?' or 'Who is empowered by the owner to determine conditions of entry?' are the only questions to be answered.

So Alan Johnson is crap-free in that episode – but not this one.

> Mr Johnson accepted that the Government's aim of getting half of young people into university by 2010 may not be met – the tally stands at 43 per cent – but he said that he was determined to 'keep the 50 per cent flame burning' . . .
>
> Emphasising Labour's 50 per cent target, Mr Johnson continued: 'If we fail in this quest, we squander human capital and waste individual potential and sell society short.'
>
> *(Alan Johnson, reported in* The Times, *15 September 2006)*

If this is your measure of squandering you can squander less by aiming at 43 per cent ('We're there boys') or if you like you can squander more by aiming at 57 per cent ('What a climb faces us, lads'). I suspect the least squandering comes at about 20 per cent, Alan, but neither of us knows, do we? That's the problem – no measuring rod in the Public Sector. But you don't seem to see that. Go back to school, but choose a private one or you'll have no measure for that either!

Nor this one – whoops, sorry Alan – it's Beverley Hughes:

> Teachers and campaigners clashed yesterday over government plans for schools to offer 'wraparound' childcare that would have pupils spending 50 hours a week in school.
>
> All schools will have to open from 8am to 6pm within the next four years in an attempt to give state school pupils the same opportunities as those in the private sector.
>
> 'Independent schools have always done this,' Ms Hughes said. 'They have given children opportunities to excel by offering them a wide range of activities.'
>
> *(Beverley Hughes, reported in* The Times, *19 September 2006)*

I can't recall, Beverley, where I read that the Government's role in education is to collect little plastic lumps of human dough from private households and shape them on the social kneading board. You want a bigger board, with the influence of parents and families receding further.

But let's be generous, Beverley, and stick to logic. So we'll forget families, and costs, and opportunity costs, and whether you're feeling deprived 'cos you only went to a grammar school, and ask you how, at the stroke of your school pen, that is going to happen? Your opponents include the leader of Britain's biggest head teachers union who accused you of turning schools into a 'national baby-sitting service'. Which they are.

Patricia Hewitt didn't learn how to do sums at wherever she was schooled:

> My Hon. Friend is absolutely right about the views of the Right Hon. Member for Witney. Indeed, let us remember that only last year he wrote the Conservative party manifesto that proposed to take millions of pounds out of the NHS for everybody and put it into subsidising private care for a few. That is what the Conservative party means by fairness.
>
> *(Patricia Hewitt, House of Commons, 11 October 2006)*

I think this is what you're on about, Blew-it:

Each year around 220,000 people without health insurance pay for important operations. We believe that providing a contribution based on the cost of half the NHS operation when people make these choices both recognises the tax they have paid towards the NHS and will help further reduce waiting lists.

(Conservative Party Election Manifesto 2006)

I'd love to see your sums, Blew-it. Here are mine:

At present, every person who leaves the NHS leaves his or her money-from-taxes *in*.

So if we all did that, the NHS would have the same huge funds without any patients: if half of us did it the same money would be there, but only half the patients! What a wonderful service you could provide.

What the Tories proposed was using *some* of the patient's money-from-taxes to pay for an operation outside the NHS. The NHS would still be better off as long as the outside cost was less than twice as much as it would cost in the NHS. You telling me you can do it at half price?

Looks like you got your 'everybody' and your 'few' precisely the wrong way round, Blew-it. Surprise, surprise.

You'd have been better off attacking the Tories' idea on other grounds. For example you could have said: 'The Tories would subsidize private patients who have no insurance – which means that people who *have* insurance (and who have equally paid the tax for no benefit) would pay double for the privilege. Then we'd watch them join the uninsured in droves!'

By the same token, Ruth (Graceless) Kelly has saved the taxpayer a mite of money by taking her son out of her hitherto beloved State Miseducation Service. But there the resemblance ends. In the same issue of *The Times* no fewer than three politicos supported her. Here is Dave the Vague:

Some people are going to say it's hypocrisy. Well, if they were going to abolish private education, then it would be hypocrisy, but they're not.

(David Cameron, reported in The Times, *9 January 2006)*

Similar remarks came from our familiar columnist David Aaronovitch and an Editorial. Yes, Dave and cronies, New Labour no longer wants to *abolish* private education à la Communism, it just wants to *control* it à la Fascism (which hardly matches your avowed 'liberal conservatism', Dave. Do you remember when you said that? Course not). First The Fat Controllers saddled private schools with a ridiculous price-fixing investigation, next they will take away their charitable status unless they take on a load of nut-cases that you can't manage (you've probably turned most of them into nut-cases) and throughout they have a deliberate policy of turning down planning applications for new private schools. You guys should *read* the papers before sounding off in them.

Yet again, Alice Miles is the only one who got it right, the next day; Graceless has 'breached the fundamental principle of the Labour party'.

Over at the National Crime Office they're fiddling while Rome burns:

> The Chief Constable of Cheshire, Peter Fahy, is appealing to the Government to change the law on positive discrimination to enable police chiefs to meet tough Home Office targets for increasing the number of black and Asian officers.
>
> *(Peter Fahy, reported by Ben Leapman, the* Daily Telegraph, *22 April 2006)*

The way they're going, all the ethnic minorities will be sent home, banged up, or in the police force.

Prisons are overcrowded, often with drug takers, but Labour knows how to deal with it:

> Communities know that crime reduction depends on drug reduction.
>
> *(Labour Party Election Manifesto 2006)*

Er, actually it doesn't, it depends on drug *prices*. No need to commit a crime for a snort if it costs no more than a pint of beer. Indeed *the pint* is more likely to lead to crime. And why does a snort cost more than a pint? Because we're in the age of Prohibition – this time of drugs. Of course there's an easier way. 'Crime reduction depends on de-criminalizing drugs'! Or if that's unpalatable, repeal the 3,000 new criminal offences that Nick Clegg (at Lib Dems conference 2006) tells us you have created since coming to power.

The Tories aren't much different; they will 'break the link between drugs and crime by massively expanding treatment programmes' (Manifesto 2005). But if they decriminalized drugs they could sell some of their prisons to rehabilitation charities too. Only one problem here; government and taxes both shrink. That would never do! Nor would allowing the public to own dangerous weapons – even though outlawing guns means that only outlaws own guns and there's plenty of evidence that crime would reduce (a decade on from the Dunblane tragedy and the tightening of gun ownership laws, gun crime is greater than ever).[3]

No, our great leaders have other ideas for our protection:

> **The best defence of our security at home is the spread of liberty and justice overseas.**
>
> *(Labour Party Election Manifesto 2005)*

Yeah right. For 'overseas' read Iraq, where bombing for a decade is supposed to make us all safer in our beds. And I was brought up to believe that charity begins at home, so how about a bit of spreading here first?

Oh but we do that too:

> **Our liberties are prized but so is our security.**
>
> *(Labour Party Election Manifesto 2005)*

Now why are these two items posed as opposites? Let me guess: because it suits Big Government. Just as you can pretend that freedom and democracy are natural friends, so you can pretend that liberty and security are natural enemies. But in reality security against terrorism means staying out of wars, having plenty of friendly informants, and allowing private institutions, including airports and airlines, to devise their own measures. It does *not* mean the obsessive collection of

---

3 See for example, *More Guns, Less Crime*, by John Lott, University of Chicago Press, Chicago, 1998.

information without regard to quality; this *distracts and hinders* the process rather than helps it. Security against internal crime means essentially the same – concentrating on prevention, not banging up a few perpetrators. Security against intrusive government means non-intrusive government – not submission, control, compliance, spying, interception, and breaking and entry. What am I missing?

Just like here, the US politicos have selective memories:

> 'America, a country of 300 million people with a GDP of $12 trillion, and more than one million soldiers and Marines, can regain control of Iraq,' the plan states.
>
> The plan (which Senior US officials say that Mr Bush is embracing) was presented to him last week by General Jack Keane, a former army vice-chief of staff, and Frederick Kagan, of the American Enterprise Institute, a conservative think-tank. The plan focuses on a military solution in Iraq, and rejects diplomacy with Iraq's neighbours.
>
> *(Reported in* The Times*, 18 December, 2006)*

In exactly the same way as Vietnam no doubt. Piece of cake.

The UK has plenty of takers, some of whom see 'mission creep' as the only proof of success. Not satisfied with Iraq, David Aaronovitch glorifies the mission in Afghanistan too:

> All the greatest missions have crept spectacularly. This is no exception . . .
>
> That's mission creep, I suppose. You go in to get rid of the Taliban and you end up risking lives just to educate women. And – both for itself, and in terms of what it means about the world we want, I think it's worth it.
>
> *(David Aaronovitch,* The Times*, 4 July 2006)*

And the Taliban, David?

Accept the spectacularly unlikely assertion that all the greatest missions have crept. Therefore any mission that creeps is great. Is that what this creep is saying? On that criterion (risking lives to educate women) where shall we send our boys next? Next door to Pakistan? Bangladesh? The Middle East? Africa?

I suppose his rigid Left–Right spectrum is to blame. But surely even David can see that cost–benefit must come in somewhere? Perhaps not – any more than Tony can; because the same *Times* (4 July) tells us that Tony Blair today promised that British troops in Afghanistan would get any additional forces they needed.

A few months later (and several more mission creeps) David's newspaper reports that five years after rebel forces marched on Kabul to oust the Taliban, 'the triumph and hope have given way to despair and disappointments' (*The Times*, 11 November 2006).

The return of the Taliban, after thousands of civilian deaths and the annihilation of the poppy trade.

There's no holding this boy down in the field of public sector binges:

> Unlike some of my colleagues at *The Times*, I am a fan of a powerful BBC, acting as the gold standard in journalism and information, as in popular entertainment. I can even accept that its executives may need to earn three or four times as much as the Prime Minister, and its senior presenters considerably more than the Deputy Prime Minister. But if its news programmes are going to become glorified scandal sheets, then I don't want to pay for it any more than I want to pay for the *Daily Mail*. Which I don't.
>
> *(David Aaronovitch, The Times, 11 July 2006)*

Difference is, David, that unlike the case of the *Daily Mail*, those who *don't* want The Beeb must pay for those who *do*. Ah well, that's democracy for you.

So here we are, back with the taxpayers. The Liberal Democrats love doling out their loot to receivers of stolen goods:

> Every pensioner couple over 75 will receive at least £167.05 per week state pension – over £140 a month more than at present. This will abolish the need for means tests altogether for a million people.
>
> *(Liberal Democrats Election Manifesto 2005)*

You can see the nonsense of this craze against means-testing if you just ask yourself 'How can we find the poor?' If you don't wish to find them then you give a State minimum benefit to *everybody* – State Pension, State Wage, the lot. Tax the division of labour until it's disappeared. Otherwise, you must have means tests – or better still, get out of the business of 'helping' the poor altogether and return the job to the charities from whom you originally pinched it. (See also Chapter 12.)

Nor can we be satisfied with merely recycling money for people to spend as they like. They have to spend it on travel:

> This means that under New Labour the richest fifth of our society get forty per cent of the public money spent on transport while the poorest fifth get just over ten per cent.
>
> You know I can't help but think that this was not quite the sort of outcome that Keir Hardie had in mind.
>
> *(Alistair Carmichael, Liberal Democrats Party Conference 2006)*

We can assume by default that these statistics are bogus. But let's take them as gospel. What's new? Who thinks that the redistribution of the Welfare State actually helps the poor? Surely nobody who has studied it over the last 60 years – at least (unlike Marx) Keir Hardie *might* have been sincere. So the question for you, Allie, is not who gets the benefit of transport subsidies, it's why *are* there any subsidies? *You*, Allie, should know that the same thing happened in the USA about 150 years ago – huge subsidies to all the 'great' railroad companies (bar one, that of James J. Hill, by far the most successful). That, and other potential interventions, is precisely why the Republican Party was formed – the promotion of private enterprise wasn't even on its radar. Ah well, put it down to a poor state education.

Perhaps Hazel (Blather) Blears knows that a State Wage is not on. But that's no obstacle – make somebody else pay it:

> We didn't introduce the National Minimum Wage simply because it is economically more efficient.
>
> We did it because it makes a difference to people's lives like the women I worked with in Tesco.
>
> *(Hazel Blears, Labour Party Conference 2006)*

Did she get the sack then? Minimum wage, maximum damage, making it unlawful to work unless you can find someone who'll pay you over the odds.

Alistair Darling decrees holidays too (and maximum hours, soon):

> We introduced the minimum wage. Increasing again next week, benefiting over 1.3 million people . . .
>
> New legislation will guarantee that staff will get bank holiday entitlement in addition to annual holidays.
>
> *(Alistair Darling, Labour Party Conference 2006)*

Why not double both? Or treble 'em? I repeat, his minimum wage has contributed to the enormous unemployment figures in this country (don't look at Government figures, which relate only to those *actively seeking a job*; in the Farewell State multiplying by five will give you a better picture). And let them choose their own hours too, including a part-time option, says Beverley Hughes (reported in *The Times* of 12 February 2007).

Any more decrees before closing time? I'm already over my maximum hours today and it's Sunday. OK we'll call it a day for now.

Appendix: Environmentalism and Energy

The Conservative Party's 'green car' stunt unveiled at its 2006 conference was a nice contradiction for Chapter 2. But the Ford Prius comparison is insufficient because, like the politicos, it assumes that energy costs can be treated as emission costs – and that they differ from other costs in the same way.

The easier point to dispose of is the latter; leaving global warming aside, there is nothing about energy which requires a different approach from all other goods. Supply is virtually infinite – 75,000 years' worth in oil alone, and limitless accessible energy in the oceans. Market prices reflect supply, demand and future changes better than any decree.

Potentially, global warming or cooling (and the extent it can be affected by man) is different, but nobody knows by how much, whether it is positive or negative, and whether warming or cooling will be (or can be made to be) a help or a hindrance on average. The science (already contaminated by government) is not up to it; the differences are too close to call. The idea of a decreed 'price' for carbon is a huge joke – the dossier is more daft than dodgy – and if an attempt is made to impose one, then another World War will be a lot nearer. As we have seen, Big Government is not queasy about war, which brings gains for government and losses for we the sheeple.

The one absolutely certain scientific fact is that the 'waste' thrown off in the refinement of raw energy is far lower under fossil fuels than it ever was under carbohydrates i.e. agriculture, simply because of the land used up by the latter. Oil is over a thousand times more frugal with land than is grain. That is why North America, for example, is already returning land to forest, which absorbs carbon, at breakneck speed, and the same goes for most developed countries.

As usual, private property rights and markets will find the best solution. This is sure to mean cleaner fuel, with oil becoming far less dominant and possibly redundant, and better climate science. Innovative markets may be able to influence temperatures, up or down, and even locally, by emissions of gas. They can take us to Antarctica, to the depths of the sea, to other planets, and may even be able to deviate the flight path of this one.

It's not just pollution (see elsewhere in this chapter) that markets and private property can deal with.

(Some references are given below.[4])

---

4 Reading matter on energy and global warming:

Climate Alarmism Reconsidered, Robert L Bradley, Institute of Economic Affairs, London, 2003.

The Bottomless Well, Peter Huber and Mark Mills, Basic Books, New York, 2005

Meltdown: The Predictable Distortion of Global Warming by Scientists, Politicians, and the Media, Patrick Michaels, Cato Institute, Washington DC, 2004.

7

Misleading Crap

Every election is a sort of advance auction of stolen goods.

(H. L. Mencken)

As in the first edition of this book, much of this chapter concerns tax-and-spend, with the politicos referring only to the 'benefits' of the spend and forgetting all about the adverse effects of the tax, which of course removes spending or investment which would have otherwise taken place.

I have a confession to make. I may be an old grump now, but at that time I was far too lenient on the politicos! We all know that they take their cut out of tax-and-spend (about 20 per cent including waste) but I hadn't appreciated a *hidden* effect which at current tax rates *removes* (into a black hole) at least two-thirds (my estimate) of the amount of the tax and spend concerned – a net loss of 67p in the pound.[1]

Basically, just like international trade tariffs, all internal taxes represent tariffs on internal trade. Only do-it-yourself (DIY) escapes. Income tax, company taxes, VAT, and all other taxes boil down to levies on internal trade (there's nothing else to tax), making a total tariff of almost 50 per cent and rising. Like tariff barriers, this serves to reduce the amount of trading and thus the division of labour, therefore lowering living standards for all. It's hidden from view, tucked away in the architecture of the economy, but there is too much DIY and not enough division of labour. For example, most travelling salesmen drive themselves around the country; lower taxes would make it economic to use specialist drivers (it is irrelevant whether the

---

1 See F. A. Hayek's *The Constitution of Liberty*, Chapter 20, Footnote 25. See also my article on 'Tax and the Division of Labour' in *Economic Affairs*, March 2003, Institute of Economic Affairs, London; this article has several references to supporting information.

salesman or the driver earns more) – thus creating more working time, and probably safer journeys to boot.

So each pound of extra tax payable has *already* inhibited the division of labour, and thus reduced output by 67p, before the tax is received. Even though government still receives its pound of flesh and spends it, the economy as a whole, *including the tax and spend*, has shrunk by 67p. (This excludes their 20 per cent cut.) Similarly every pound of tax-*relief* produces a further 67p to the economy as a whole. (These are my estimates; I suggest not incredible when one remembers that 100 per cent total tax would lead to no division of labour at all!)

Please bear this in mind for all that follows.

The more that people catch on to this, the more desperate the politicos will get, which perhaps explains the fact that 'misleading' gets closer and closer to out and out lying. As politics gets bigger, so does its immorality and corruption.

Not that Misleading Crap wasn't alive and well in 1975. Ted Heath was in top form; here he is proudly pointing to the part his government played in Mencken's auction:

> Let those who read our manifesto also read there the pledge we gave that we would have an advanced regional policy that we would never allow the regions to go on suffering as they have done in the past.
>
> *(Edward Heath, Conservative Party Conference 1973)*

Anticipating that some idiot like me would blurt out 'which regions?' his chum Peter Walker gave the answer:

> In the Northern region we have in this past year reduced unemployment by nearly 30,000. We have created directly 10,000 new jobs. We are considering proposals that will create another 9,000 jobs. We have allocated 19 advance factories . . . We have brought more economic vitality to the North than any past Labour Government.
>
> *(Peter Walker, Conservative Party Conference 1973)*

I hope that my response to this illustrates the 'unseen' consequences of all boasts along these lines:

'And taken more away from the other regions, where by these same actions you have increased unemployment by nearly 30,000, taken away 10,000 potential new jobs, and are considering taking away another 9,000. The money you took from us to finance these projects is money which would otherwise have been spent creating jobs. More productive jobs than you, in fact, because there would have been no parasitic bureaucracy in between and because it would have been spent in making things which consumers wanted rather than what you think they should have.'

This same old stuff still does the rounds:

> My Hon. Friend makes a good case. He agrees that his entire region has been transformed under this Labour Government, with massive new investment, huge numbers of new jobs and a booming economy.
> *(Peter Hain, House of Commons, 15 February 2006)*

This concerned the benefits bestowed on Deeside and taken away from everywhere else.

You can play this trick on the uninitiated with pretty well any activity you like.

Here's another from 1975:

> We shall gradually extend free nursery schooling throughout the country so that within ten years it should be available for all three and four year old children whose parents wish them to have it . . .
> We will defend the fundamental right of parents to spend their money on their children's education should they wish to do so.
> *(Conservative Party Election Manifesto February 1974)*

Was my response fair?

'Unless of course the stingy so-and-so's want to spend nothing. (What's that – they'd rather spend their time even if it means giving up work, 'cos they can do more with their kids than the lousy teachers can? Shut up.) As we were saying, if they want to spend nothing, they'll still have to pay us to provide the free services for the children of less 'selfish' parents.'

Parents become more and more redundant by the day. Supernanny takes their money and spends it on the kids: For better or worse:

> Expert opinion confirms what common sense tells us: children well taught and well-cared-for in their early years have a better opportunity to lead successful and rewarding lives. The Government has the wrong priorities, handing out a one-off cash windfall to 18-year-olds at taxpayers' expense through the Child Trust Fund. Liberal Democrats will use this money better by recruiting 21,000 more teachers to cut infant class sizes from the present maximum of 30 to an average of 20 and junior class sizes to an average of 25. We will extend before and after school provision from 8 a.m. to 6 p.m. for all children and complete 3500 Children's Centres by 2010.
>
> *(Liberal Democrats Election Manifesto 2005)*

Is that so? Why is it, then, that the highest reading levels at age 9 and 14 are associated with a starting age of around seven?[2]

Perish the thought that home is better than Supernanny's schools. Defer the damage as long as you can. And get out when you've had enough – as education specialist Professor Alison Wolf says in the *Financial Times* of 17 January 2006, apropos Alan Johnson's proposal to enforce school attendance until age 18 unless in other formal training: 'Mr Johnson believes he will be helping teenagers into work. But there is very clear evidence about what most promotes long-term employment; and it is getting a job.'

For Ruth Kelly the thought that Mum knows best was never a starter as far as we the sheeple are concerned:

> In last week's Budget, we had to make a choice – we could invest in our children, schools and young people or we could put tax cuts before the needs of our young people.
>
> *(Ruth Kelly, House of Commons, 27 March 2006)*

You mean 'before letting the people choose' – as they did, and paid for, so successfully until 1870 (see Chapter 4). Didn't they teach you that at Westminster School?

And I don't suppose you know that over the pond (rather like the nurses here – see Chapter 5) a survey of the Chicago area showed that

---

2 See the paper written by Caroline Sharp in 1997 for the National Foundation for Education Research.

22 per cent of school children attend private schools, but 46 per cent of government school teachers' kids do. A New York survey showed no member of the Board of Education and no citywide elected official had children in government schools.

And what's this about investment anyway?

> The economic imperative of education, training and skills is clear and real . . .
>
> *(Ruth Kelly, Association of Colleges Conference, 16 November 2005)*

Here is what a real education specialist (Alison Wolf again, not a bird of passage moving from one department to another) says:

> An unquestioning faith in the economic benefits of education has brought with it huge amounts of wasteful government spending, attached to misguided and even pernicious policies.[3]

But Ruth Kelly is on to the waste like a flash:

> I am delighted that we have appointed Caroline Lewis as chair for the Bureaucracy Reduction Group. I look to her to be relentless in hunting down unnecessary red tape.
>
> *(Ruth Kelly, Association of Colleges Conference, 16 November 2005)*

Our Ruth has form on red tape in her new job (Secretary of State, Department for Communities and Local Government – yes, ridiculous isn't it?); one of the first things she did was to launch a Commission. What else? Most of the members in the Public Sector. What else?

We'll meet Lord Sainsbury later. In the meantime one of his businessmen knows what will happen next:

> If there is one thing I have learned over my forty years in the property business, it is that you cannot trust a local authority, government body or any tier of their bureaucracy to proceed with an agreed matter unless it is bound contractually by a water-tight

---

3 *Does Education Matter?* Professor Alison Wolf, Penguin Books, 2002.

contract, and even then, if large enough amounts are involved, the rules can be changed to enable bureaucrats to wriggle out of commitments they have made (as they did, you will recall, in the case of Railtrack).

(Andrew Perloff, Chairman, Panther Securities plc, Annual Report 2005)

Ruth's successor, Alan (Smoothie) Johnson, is even worse than Ruth:

In the very worst cases, where children are at real danger, or where the parents may be abusive, violent or extremely ill; the state has to intervene to take that child into care.

These children are all too often let down by their family, only for the state to let them down even more. Looked after children are five times less likely to pass five good GCSEs and twenty-five times more likely to end up in custody as an adult.

(Alan Johnson's speech to The National Family and Parenting Institute, 25 July 2006)

Not the best grammar you've ever seen is it? But horrific education results should be the least of your worries as this book goes to press. As reported in *The Times* of 26 January 2007, a group of MPs claim that children are being taken into care and then recycled, simply to meet adoption targets. This could be the mother of all in-care scandals, and they're not in short supply, Alan. Shouldn't you be considering whether the same might be true throughout the Farewell State, including the State Education system. Oh, that's not the way government works, is it? Pity.

Gaily accepting the Supernanny fable nevertheless, Smoothie has a money tree:

This revolution in Britain's workplaces, homes and families has benefited millions of parents, hundreds of thousands of children . . .

(Alan Johnson's speech to The National Family and Parenting Institute, 25 July 2006)

As usual the 'revolution' was old fashioned tax and spend. Take and give and forget the take – a forced transfer from non-parents. (Who else? Children? Santa Claus?)

Nor does Supernanny's grip relax as the kids grow up:

> No more dropping out at 16.
> We will not let economic disadvantage stand in the way of young people staying in education beyond the age of 16.
>
> *(Labour Party Election Manifesto 2005)*

Will you force them to stay in, then? As reported in *The Times* of 12 January 2006, we have the answer, from Alan Johnson and Flash Gordo: Yes.

We mustn't forget the grown-ups so we'll spend on them too. On goes Mencken's auction:

> We are now putting in place a comprehensive and ambitious strategy to help everyone get on at work.
> All adults to get free access to basic skills in literacy, language and numeracy.
>
> *(Labour Party Election Manifesto 2005)*

Now it's getting a little clearer – we actually see the word tax appearing:

> Government cannot shirk its responsibilities. Our starting point is that for children to come first parents need to be given choices: a tax and benefit system to raise family incomes and tackle child poverty.
> We are also committed to making work pay – with a guaranteed income of at least £258 per week for those with children in full-time work.
>
> *(Labour Party Election Manifesto 2005)*

Can the Tories trump that? They can if we forget the tax:

> During the next Parliament, we will ensure that all working families who qualify for the working tax credit will receive up to £50 a week for each child under the age of five, irrespective of the type of childcare they choose.
>
> *(Conservative Party Election Manifesto 2005)*

And they've still got something left over for the oldies:

> Our new, permanent discount, reducing council tax bills by up to
> £500 for households where all residents are over 65 will be fully
> funded by central government.
>   A Conservative Government will increase the basic state pension
> in line with earnings rather than prices, reversing the spread of
> means testing.
>
> *(Conservative Party Election Manifesto 2005)*

Wow. Well done; you won this auction. Labour will only do that in
2012 – or never.

Or did they?

> All pensioners have benefited from improved universal benefits
> like the state pension, the Winter Fuel Payment (now worth £300
> per year for the over-80s), help with council tax and free TV licences
> for the over 75s. This year all households expected to pay council
> tax that include anyone over 65 will receive £200 towards the cost
> of council tax, and the following year there will be free, off-peak
> local bus travel in England for the over-60s.
>
> *(Labour Party Election Manifesto 2005)*

In the land of the free, the Democrats manage *double* deception with
ease. Taxes will be cut *and* they'll be up there with best in the largesse
auction:

> We will cut taxes for 98 percent of Americans . . .

Then they'll invest in cities and towns, businesses, schools, hospitals
(of course!), help with cost of living increases and be:

> absolutely committed to preserving Social Security. It is a compact
> across the generations.
>
> *(US Democratic Party Platform 2004)*

Sorry to spoil the party's party but your compact isn't a contract (see
Chapter 9).

What else do we expect from political auctions, given the lack of funds dedicated to specific purposes?

Yes, they can print some 'money' – which simply devalues all the rest.

Yes, they can borrow to finance the difference between income and expenses, but that's called mortgaging the future, in this case future generations – you know, those yet to be born who will be overwhelmed by climate change. You want us to pay for that in taxes, whilst you carry on borrowing from them for all your boondoggles. Right now that's about $75,000 per head (of current population) in the USA and of the same order in the UK. And it's growing by the day. The USA bill for the Iraq war (as at end 2006) is about $3,000 per household.

A lot of liability to dump on the little ones. Well *I* think so. But not the politicos. Not the US Republicans, that's for sure – their 2004 platform calls it 'unwelcome but manageable'.

Just like home in fact. Why shouldn't the Lib Dems make a bid? All's fair in politics and war. But they maintain that they're above this sort of thing:

> Unlike the other parties, we have consistently set out costings for our manifesto pledges, explaining how much money they will need and how they will all be paid for. So this manifesto includes a specific section outlining our main costings.
>
> *(Liberal Democrats Election Manifesto 2005)*

Just so. You'd expect that a genuine liberal would let us decide what's affordable seeing it's our money.

But I jest; let's be serious. What you'd think is that a 'specific section outlining our costings' would be in the list of 11 sections on the first page of the manifesto. But it's not. It's a measly little box (a quarter of a page out of 20 pages) and it's worse than useless. It wouldn't pass muster as a corporate business plan. On top of this, 'Green Action' sections take more than 2 pages and aren't costed at all.

I can see what Mencken meant. I can also see what Frederic Bastiat meant when he said 'The State is the great fictitious entity by which everyone seeks to live at the expense of everyone else'.

Tax and spend on the youngsters. Tax and spend on those of working age. Tax and spend on the oldies. (And spend on the shysters.)

Who's been missed out? The sick? With the NHS around, the likely-to-be-made-sick is nearer the mark. But our Dave loves it:

> My family is so often in the hands of the NHS. And I want them to be safe there.
>
> *(David Cameron, Conservative Party Conference 2006)*

And they will – by fast track! As is well known any politician (or pal) or any doctor (or pal) has no problem.

Meanwhile, Patricia Hewitt is ill:

Patricia Hewitt is suffering from a medical condition in which she says the opposite of what is true. Those close to the Health Secretary accept this and have learnt to cope. So when Pat says 'the sun is shining' they know that, in fact, it is bucketing down and to take an umbrella.

(Reported by Ann Treneman, The Times, 8 March 2006)

If all the journalists at *The Times* were like Ann Treneman this book would be considerably shorter. But they aren't.

Sports writer Matthew Syed is dodgy outside his field. As on 20 July 2006 when he tears into George Bush (not for the war in Iraq, as Chief Sports Writer Martin Samuel does brilliantly) but for blocking proposals to lift funding restrictions on stem cell research. Let it rip, never mind other priorities eh Matthew? Of course the issue is *taxpayer-funded* research; nobody is stopping the private sector doing it. Indeed the 'stem-cell breakthrough', which was *The Times'* main headline on

24 August 2006, was made by a private company, just as were countless other breakthroughs including the discovery of penicillin.

Alistair Darling takes our money for *his* science indulgences:

> We have more than doubled our science budget to almost three and half billion pounds per year, supporting new research and development for example in stem cells and nanotechnology . . .
>
> We've invested over £3bn to make sure that our scientists have modern facilities . . .
>
> *(Alistair Darling, Labour Party Conference 2006)*

In June 2006 Lord Sainsbury, the former Science and Innovation minister, called for the Government to spend more (and therefore to filch more) on applied research *to meet the needs of business!* Now there's chutzpah.

And here is real public sector science:

> Ministers and environmental campaigners have been urged to use spin to persuade the public to tackle climate change.
>
> *Warm Words*, a report by the Institute for Public Policy Research [IPPR], a left-wing think-tank, advised them to act as if there were no dispute over the causes and rate of climate change.
>
> *(Reported in* The Times, *3 August 2006)*

For dodgy arguments, attack is the best form of defence. Like our own Chris Huhne of the Lib Dems in Chapter 5, the US Democrats have really cottoned on to that:

> And even though overwhelming scientific evidence shows that global climate change is a scientific fact, this administration has rewritten government reports to hide that fact.
>
> *(US Democratic Party Platform 2004)*

The one thing we can all be clear about is that this dispute has lots of protagonists on both sides – the broad split being between the politicos and the proper scientists. Trust the form.

Those who disagree with the politicos should lose their liberties, says Margaret Beckett. No messin':

On Thursday [9 November 2006] Margaret Beckett, the Foreign Secretary, compared climate sceptics to advocates of Islamic terror. Neither, she said, should have access to the media.

(Reported in Sunday Telegraph, *12 November)*

The public sector rolls on merrily (and illiberally), undeterred by failures. Here's John Reid on the bursting prisons crisis (explaining the plan to offer foreign prisoners money to go home to serve their sentences):

It isn't true to paint this as a crisis.

(John Reid, reported in The Times, *10 October 2006)*

As another example of what first woke me up to all this crap (see the Introduction), on 13 February 2006 (heralding further legislation) Gordon Brown said:

No-one should be able to publicly celebrate and glorify what happened in London last July and walk away from the consequences.

(Gordon Brown's speech to the Royal United Services Institute,
13 February 2006)

But as Peter Oborne remarked later in *The Spectator*, there is already a perfectly good and serviceable piece of law which deals with the problem; the Offences against the Person Act of 1861, which is still in force and outlaws incitement to violence and murder.

The politicos don't want to *seem* repressive and who could be more sweetly reasonable than Charles Clarke on identity cards?

I don't think there is any benefit in opting out at all, said Mr Clarke, who called yesterday a 'red letter day' for his department. Anyone who opts out, in my opinion, is foolish . . . Being able to prove who we are is a fundamental requirement in modern society.

(Charles Clarke, reported in the Daily Telegraph, *31 March 2006)*

Prove to whom, pray? And with you lot in charge there will soon be so much theft that anyone up to no good will have several identity cards – none of them their own!

It may be worse in the land of the free. In June 2006 in Guantanamo Bay, three internees – or prisoners, or detainees, or whatever you want to call human beings jailed indefinitely without conviction and with no hope of legal recourse – committed suicide. Here are a couple of reactions from the neocons:

> The camp's commander Rear Admiral Harry B. Harris described the detainees' decision as 'an act of asymmetrical warfare.' The Deputy Assistant of State Colleen Graffy classed the deaths as 'a good PR move.' And Southcom commander General Bantz J. Craddock commented that, 'This may be an attempt to influence the judicial proceedings' of a case now pending before the U.S. Supreme Court about the President's ad hoc military commissions.'
>
> *(Reported by TomPaine.com, The Guantánamo Peril, 19 June 2006)*

Meanwhile, George Bush has unconstitutionally suspended habeas corpus on the basis that 'we are protecting Americans'. So, as explained by James Abourezk in the USA political newsletter *Counterpunch*, there is now no way to learn whether or not the prisoner is an enemy or just someone who was gathered up in a sweep of foreigners in Afghanistan, because, without habeas corpus, their detention cannot be tested in a court.

And if you think the Democratic Party will be any better, one of the words NOT featuring in their 2004 Platform (nor the Republicans', of course) is 'Guantanamo', where hundreds of prisoners of America still languish without hope. As I said, the land of the free.

To finish this chapter, let's come back home to where we came in, taxes and 'the regions' where Douglas Alexander is preening himself in his public sector cocoon. Asked whether he agreed with the new head of the CBI, Richard Lambert, in saying the especially large public sector in Scotland is a constraint on the growth of its economy, he replied:

> Candidly, I do not agree with that observation, for the following reasons. First, there is no direct correlation between the size of the public sector and the level of economic growth not just in Scotland but, indeed, in other European countries. For decades, Scandinavian countries, for example, have had a large public sector, along

with high and sustained employment. Secondly, it is time that the Opposition left behind the rather tired and familiar argument of 'Private sector, good; public sector, bad'. The recipe for modern economic success relies on effective research and development, along with effective vocational skills and education, all of which is contingent on the sustained economic investment in the public sector achieved under the Labour Government.

(Douglas Alexander, Secretary of State for Transport,
House of Commons, 4 July 2006)

Candid maybe, *but not on the issue raised i.e. growth*. Soviet Russia had high and sustained employment – alongside dreadfully deteriorating living standards. Sweden's economy (is that the one you mean?) has never fully recovered from a public sector orgy between 1950 (public sector lower than the USA) and 1975, and is now well down the list of well-off countries. But the orgy is reversing and its overall tax burden is now lower than that of the UK. And 'burden' is the right word, Duggie. The inverse relationship between living standards and the size of the public sector is well documented in theory (as in the introduction to this chapter) and practice, including ongoing worldwide studies at the Heritage Foundation, the Fraser Institute and even the World Bank.

Preen on Duggie, we're paying for you but we're not listening. Politicians talk, we pay. Instead we're wondering how much our living standards are affected when for every pound you extort from us the country loses a net 67p, straight down the plug'ole. (Better than up into that perilously thin air, your next excuse for more plunder of we the people.) But that's for another day.

8

Ideological Crap

In Washington there isn't any plan
With 'feeding David' on page sixty-four;
It must be accidental that the milk man
Leaves a bottle at my door.

It must be accidental that the butcher
Has carcasses arriving at his shop
The very place where, when I need some meat,
I accidentally stop.

My life is chaos turned miraculous;
I speak a word and people understand
Although it must be gibberish since words
Are not produced by governmental plan.

Now law and order, on the other hand
The state provides us for the public good;
That's why there's instant justice on demand
And safety in every neighbourhood.

(The Machinery of Freedom, *David Friedman*)

David Friedman is even more radical about small government than his father Milton, the world-famous economist who died at the age of ninety-four in November 2006.

Should government be large or small? Statism versus Individualism, not Left versus Right, is the Big Issue.

In fact as Hugh Dalton, then Labour Chancellor of Exchequer, said in 1945, 'Once upon a time, three hundred years ago, the City of London was a stronghold of Radicalism, an outpost of the Left'. The Right versus Left terminology appears to have come from little more than a seating plan in the French Assemblies of 1789 and there is no doubt that Right represented Authority (anything but free markets) and Left meant radical change in favour of individual liberty in all its forms. So I'm a left-winger – great!

Big Government is imperialist as well as welfarist. It has to be because state welfare policies lead to protectionism and hence war. Only free trade (is that Right or Left?) is compatible with peace. Historians have long recognized the fusion of Bismarckism, Fascism and National Socialism. To the German nationalists only one 'freedom' counted – freedom from importing food. George Bernard Shaw found no difficulty in praising the domestic policies of Hitler, Stalin, Mussolini (who hopped from 'Left' to 'Right' in the twinkling of an eye) and Oswald Mosley.

Unfortunately the prevailing ideology remains Big Government, whether it is to fight wars or promote the Farewell State:

> I have spoken of a new concept of public service, which may not sound a short-term matter at all. What I have in mind is a delineation of essential public services from other services; a boundary line between hospitals and department stores, or the post office and the head office of an insurance company; and a clear commitment that essential public services will be provided at all times.

This is so, so David Cameron, but it is actually from the previous edition of this book; Professor Ralf Dahrendorf giving the Reith Lectures in 1974.

Who decides what are 'essential public services'? The politicos cry out in unison 'whatever they are at present and then some more'.

But public services start with an enormous disadvantage; outside private enterprise, profit–loss calculation is simply unavailable. The *only* alternative is to operate under detailed rules and targets. See also the Appendix at the end of this chapter.

The politicos plough on regardless:

> [We'll show] that the way to build public services for the 21st century is to trust people and share responsibility.
>
> *(Francis Maude, Party Chairman, Conservative Party Conference 2006)*

You can trust us, Francis, but why should we trust *you*? We're already sharing all we produce with you – on a 50/50 basis. And your services get worse and worse.

Will an 'instinctive liberal' get us out of the mess? In *The Times* of 6 July 2006 Anatole Kaletsky, an Associate Editor of the newspaper, described himself as 'an instinctive liberal who believes that private initiative generally delivers better results than public spending'. Sounds good – but surely he's not changing the habits of a lifetime:

> The first flaw is the one I discussed last week: the loss of focus on the core responsibilities of government – the tasks that must be undertaken by the State because they cannot be left to individuals co-operating though private markets. These range from the law enforcement to poverty alleviation, environmental protection, the promotion of public culture and the financing of pure scientific research.
>
> *(Anatole Kaletsky,* The Times, *4 May 2006)*

Bit dodgy, Anatole. Your favoured suppliers, nay, your *only possible suppliers,* didn't do too well over 'alleviating poverty' in the last century and this one's looking worse. Your 'pure scientific research' again your *only possible supplier*, has contaminated its science beyond repair, while the Vice-Chancellor of Buckingham University in an article in your own paper (5 June 2006) tells us that 'Science is not a field of endeavour on which taxpayers' money need be spent'.

George Reisman goes even further, arguing that

> This epistemological breakdown [of contemporary science] radic-ally accelerated, starting practically on the very day in the 1960s when the government took over most of the scientific research in the United States and began the large scale financing of statistical studies as a substitute for the discovery of causes.
>
> *(George Reisman in* Capitalism: A Treatise on Economics,
> *Ottawa, Illinois, Jameson Books 1996)*

Amen to that, in the UK too.

At least Kaletsky didn't have education on his list. Despite the state's offering at a NIL price at the point of use, which in the private sector would be 'predatory pricing' *par excellence* and a criminal offence, the private sector thrives. But for how long?

> Independent schools must offer more scholarships and bursaries to enable greater numbers of children from poor families to benefit from the 'dream' of a private education, a leading headmaster said yesterday.
>
> Such generosity is vital if independent schools are to see off challenges to their charitable status, suggested Rowland Constantine, chairman of the Incorporated Association of Preparatory Schools (IAPS).
>
> *(Rowland Constantine, reported in* The Times, *26 September 2006)*

Similar sentiments come from Sir Cyril Taylor, Chairman of the Specialist Schools and Academies Trust and something of a School Czar:

> Britain's 2,500 independent schools are providing excellent education to some 620,000 children, saving the taxpayer some £2.1 billion of State expenditure . . .
>
> But in order to justify their charitable status, they can and should help all our children to receive a decent education.
>
> *(Sir Cyril Taylor, Brighton Independent Schools Conference, 12 May 2005)*

Is this chutzpah or what? The £2.1 billion a year that independent schools save the taxpayers is about twenty-five times their tax relief! 'Our' Government is now plotting, aided and abetted by other Czars, to filch even more – or else. If I were Sir Cyril Taylor I'd be telling them – and Rowland Constantine – to get stuffed. Or to give this public-spirited little group of 'our' parents refunds of the full costs of a State education. Or at the very least full tax relief thereon.

Are there some other vested interests around here somewhere? I only ask.

The Culture Minister wants to rewrite history:

> The film version of *The History Boys* reminds us that teaching the past remains a battleground. The latest shot has been fired by David Lammy, the Culture Minister, who suggests that the history

of slavery be made a compulsory part of the national curriculum to
mark Britain's abolition of the slave trade . . .

(David Lammy, reported by Mick Hume, The Times, *20 October 2006)*

What almost certainly wouldn't be taught about the anti-slavery
movement is that free-market economists (led by John Stuart Mill)
were very much to the fore and that most of the supposedly reformist
writers (warmongers Carlyle and Ruskin, Kingsley, and even Charles
Dickens) were very much in the rear, not to put too fine a point on it.
(A major exception was Thomas Hughes.)

In the land of the free, compulsory and mainly nationalized education was introduced for very similar ideological reasons as in the UK
and has fared no better if this report is anything to go by:

As far as egalitarian goals go, the state system does a horrible job.
Even its most vehement supporters would scarcely claim that public
schools offer equal quality of education across socioeconomic lines.
Jencks (1985) declares, 'the annual expenditure per pupil in a pros-
perous suburb is usually at least fifty percent more than in a slum in
the same metropolitan area . . . taxpayers typically spend less than
$5,000 [per pupil, per year] for the formal education of most slum
children compared to more than $10,000 for many suburban
children.' Also, the statist system has failed to equalize primary education along racial lines. Coleman and Hoffer (1987, p. xxiv) found
in private schools less racial segregation than their public counterparts. Furthermore, public education, even on average, is far from
high quality. The National Assessment of Educational Progress
reports that 50 percent of all high school seniors in America could
not answer this question:

Which of the following is true about 87% of 10?

a. It is greater than 10;
b. It is less than 10;
c. It is equal to 10;
d. Can't tell.

*(*Enterprising Education: Doing Away with the Public School System,
Andrew Young and Walter Block, Mises Institute, 19 August 2006, www.mises.org)

So it's all been in vain – poor education and negative social engineering. Yet the cries for more continue; failed ideology imposed on the sheeple.

It hardly seems fair to examine the NHS. But Cameron is irresistible. He has a magic wand in the shape of an NHS Independence Bill, taking politicians out of the day-to-day running of the NHS. Pity you limit it to day-to-day; if you really left it alone it would be sold off, hospital by hospital. Lolly for you to slash taxes and genuine health care for us.

But it's your Clause 4, David:

> We believe that everyone has the right to high quality health care, free at the point of use.
>
> *(Conservative Party Election Manifesto 2005)*

But the wand won't work. That's why you have these agencies like NICE, telling you (as if you didn't know) that all 'health' matters *cannot* be free at the point of use – it costs you a helluva lot even to *get to* the point of use nowadays! Often hundreds of miles away, I'm told. And hundreds of treatments, operations, and pieces of equipment are off limits because they cost too much.

If anything could convince a politico that 'planning' at government level can't work, surely it is the broken NHS. Yes, 'planning' is required. We all plan every day, and our plans are coordinated every day by the miracle of prices; the issue is *government* planning.

Take homes, for example. Here's Ruth (Graceless) Kelly:

> We have committed to provide 75,000 additional social rented homes between 2004–05 and 2007–08, and social housing will be a Government priority in the current comprehensive spending review.
>
> This is in the context of our ambition, as announced in the Government's response to the Barker review last December, to increase the overall supply of housing in England – market as well as affordable homes – to 200,000 per year over the next decade.
>
> *(Ruth Kelly, House of Commons, 6 June 2006)*

Social housing? Does this really mean *anti*-social housing, on estates where it's not safe to go out at night – and often in the day time either? And, Ruth, either your grammar is dreadful or you're suggesting that 'market' homes are unaffordable. Must be a lot of surplus stock then!

It wasn't like that in the old days though – or at least it wasn't going to be. This is from the first edition of this book:

> Social ownership will bring the prospect of a home in proper repair with modern amenities and security within it.
>
> *(Fabian Society pamphlet 'The end of the Private Landlord'*
> *September 1973 – Guardian, 10 September 1973)*

And so the magic wand came out in Labour's Manifesto at the time:

> Everybody is entitled to a decent home at a price they can afford. This cannot be achieved in a free-for-all market, which has resulted in homelessness, over-crowding and squalor for thousands of our people.
>
> *(Labour Party Election Manifesto October 1974)*

At that time I referred to the many years of social ownership and rent controls; there *was* no 'free-for-all' market. (There was no free market either; a free market is not a free-for-all – it rests on enforceable private property rights.)

And as for the Barker review, it seems a moderately sensible document given the Czarist approach, but it's the Czarist approach that's the problem. As Gabriel Rozenberg points out in *The Times* of 11 December 2006, 'house-building in Britain is run along Soviet lines: the great planning system, a child of the Attlee era, rules all . . .'[1] In particular supply is permanently reduced by two major features – the control of land-use and control of rents.

Railways are another example. We needn't take too long over John Prescott's post-1997 election boast that 'I will have failed in five years time if there are not many more people using public transport and far

---

1 Rozenberg also points out that less than ten per cent of the land in England is developed.

fewer journeys by car. It's a tall order, but I urge you to hold me to it'.

Ha ha. Two-Jags John started all over again in 2000 with his now infamous ten-year plan for an 'integrated transport policy' – as elusive as ever when Stephen Byers replaced him and as elusive as ever now with Alistair Darling at the helm.

The Lib Dems want to plan transport too; their 2005 Manifesto says, 'Good transport in all forms is vital to a successful economy' (Amen to that, I say) – 'yet governments, both Tory and Labour, have failed to deliver it.'

Who is surprised? We *don't need a 'transport policy'* or a Transport Minister.[2] Send 'em packing, by road or rail or sea or air; just get rid.

I wish I could say the land of the free is better. It isn't. How about this for a Bushie? This one's on energy:

> We must also change how we power our automobiles. We will increase our research in better batteries for hybrid and electric cars and in pollution-free cars that run on hydrogen. We'll also fund additional research in cutting-edge methods of producing ethanol, not just from corn but from wood chips and stalks or switch grass. Our goal is to make this new kind of ethanol practical and competitive within 6 years.
>
> Breakthroughs on this and other new technologies will help us reach another great goal: To replace more than 75 percent of our oil imports from the Middle East by 2025.
>
> *(George W Bush, State of the Union Address, 31 January 2006)*

Irwin Stelzer has a few details – and a good answer:

> If the president has his way, the government will invest in a variety of alternative technologies. His list includes: $281m already targeted for clean coal technologies is to be brought forward; $54m will be spent to develop pollution-free coal plants that capture and store carbon emissions; $148m is devoted to a Solar America Initiative; $44m will go for wind-energy research; $150m to help

---

2 See *Transport Policy: the Myth of Integrated Planning*, Professor John Hibbs, Hobart Paper 140. Institute of Economic Affairs, London, 2000.

develop bio-based transport fuels from agricultural waste products such as 'wood chips and stalks or switch grass'.

There are more bits and pieces, but you get the idea: little projects resulting from big-government thinking, all sharing a fatal flaw. The central planners in the White House and the Department of Energy have decided which technologies hold the greatest promise, and are prepared to spend other people's money to find out if they can do a better job than markets in allocating resources to technologies that might, just might, yield alternatives to oil.

(Irwin Stelzer, Sunday Times, 5 February 2006)

The US Democrats are miles behind:

With sixty-five percent of the world's oil reserves in the Middle East, we cannot drill our way to energy independence. But we can create, think, imagine, and invent our way there.

(US Democratic Party Platform 2004)

Well, a couple of years behind. No doubt they'll have caught up by now because their platform also boasts 'It's this simple: When we see a problem, we roll up our sleeves and solve it.' Just like Ted Heath and John Reid (see Introduction).

On energy, George Reisman had the best answer in 2001:

Today, it is possible once again to bring about a dramatic fall in the price of oil – indeed, one even larger than occurred in the 1980s. And it could begin right away. All that is necessary is to abolish the U.S. government's restrictions on domestic energy production inspired by the environmentalist movement . . .

Every barrel of oil that the environmentalists have succeeded in getting the U.S. government not to allow to be produced, every ton of coal that they have prevented from being mined, every atomic power plant whose construction they have stopped, has served to make oil scarcer and more expensive and subsequently to enrich OPEC and increase the funds available for the support of terrorism.

('Free Markets Would Be OPEC's Undoing', Mises Institute, 18 September 2001)

And if Europe can make it worse it certainly will:

> Jose Manuel Barroso, the President of the Commission, said:
>
> 'We are proposing a common strategy for energy. We are in a new energy century. Demand is rising. Europe's reserves are declining. There is underinvestment and our climate is changing. We must have an approach to match this new reality – the EU can no longer afford 25 different and uncoordinated energy policies.'
>
> *(Jose-Manuel Barroso, reported in* The Times, *9 March 2006)*

And our UK supremo (presumably in his ignorance) caves in:

> Malcolm Wicks, the Energy Minister, welcomed the Commission's proposals yesterday. He said:
>
> 'We are entering into a new energy era where the world's regions are dependent on each other for ensuring energy security. No longer can energy policy be created by each EU member state in complete isolation. By speaking with the same voice, towards the same goals, the Union can achieve its energy goals for the benefit of all EU citizens.'
>
> *(Malcolm Wicks, reported in* The Times, *9 March 2006)*

May I translate?

- Markets – worst of all
- Individual Governments – bad
- Union of Government – good
- And thus? World Government – best?

I just can't get my head around why things worked so much better without central planning! How language developed without Government (remember Esperanto?) – as well as gas and electricity, transport, courts, police, education, hospitals, caring for the poor, dictionaries, accounting; the list is endless. Yet the Home Office can't even get its own departments to work together or even talk to each other.

How many times have you read a government response to a fiasco that advocates retreat or repeal? The very best they can do is 'replace' – for example the not-fit-for-purpose Child Support Agency becomes Child Maintenance and Enforcement Commission – in 2008!

If we don't quite need a world government on energy, we certainly do on the environment and global warming, don't we?

> We are imprisoned by our political Hippocratic Oath: we will deliver unto the electorate more goodies than anybody else. Such an oath was only ever achievable by increasing our despoliation of the world's resources. Our economic model is not so different in the cold light of day to that of the Third Reich – which knew it could only expand by grabbing what it needed from its neighbours.
>
> Genocide followed. Now there is a case to answer that genocide is once again an apt description of how we are pursuing business as usual, wilfully ignoring the consequences for the poorest people in the world.
>
> *(Colin Challen, Chairman, All-Party Parliamentary Climate Change Group)*

I've just a couple of problems on that, Colin. (I'm ignoring your elevation of grubby election auctions to 'Hippocratic Oath'.) In the first place I haven't quite gotcha on the poorest people bit. How does that square up with Bjorn Lomborg's calculation[3] that the cost of *one year* of Kyoto would be enough to eradicate contaminated water for ever, all over the world? Or are we just going to pull up the drawbridge?

In the second place I don't think much of your history. Yes, the Third Reich needed to grab from its neighbours – *because* it had already decided to pursue self-sufficiency and not trade, and for no other reason. But the Third Reich believed implicitly in 'protecting the environment' and indeed in 1935 enacted a law intended to do just that. Like a number of current environmentalists, it had contempt for the lives of other human beings.

It's not as if we haven't got enough war and terrorism in the world, especially with Bush still around:

---

3 Bjorn Lomborg, *Daily Telegraph*, 9 May 2004.

We will fight them in Iraq; we will fight them across the world; we will stay and fight until the fight has been won . . .

(George Bush, reported in The Times, 21 March 2006)

This is the man who suspends (almost certainly indefinitely) all manner of individual liberties and protection at home to ram down the throats of any country which doesn't provide enough 'liberty' (aka 'democracy') to its own people.

Tony Blair could hardly make it plainer that war is the health of the state:

> There are two types of nations similar to ours today; those who do war fighting and peacekeeping and those who . . . have retreated to peacekeeping alone. Britain does both.
>
> *(Tony Blair, speaking in Plymouth on 12 January 2007)*

Tony Blair's heir-apparent Gordon Brown is rattling the same sabre – at home:

> I think any preaching of religious or racial hatred will offend mainstream opinion in this country and I think we have got to do whatever we can to root it out from whatever quarter it comes. And if that means we have got to look at the laws again, we will have to do so.
>
> *(Gordon Brown, reported in* The Times, *11 November 2006)*

This came after a legal action against the Chairman of the British National Party for condemning Islam as a 'wicked, vicious faith' had failed.

Voltaire wouldn't have felt safe with Flash Gordon – it would be incitement to say 'I may not like what you say, but I will defend to the death your right to say it'.

And death it might have been.

I was hoping to give the Farewell State a miss in this chapter although it's an ideology if ever there was one and it's crap. It's having a good run in the book as a whole and of course its tentacles include health and education. So I'll make do with just one example – anyone who writes to me can have more!

> We know that parents and young people think that there should be more things to do and places to go for teenagers. We will publish plans to reform provision in order to ensure that all young people have access to a wider set of activities after the school day such as sport and the arts.
>
> *(Labour Party Election Manifesto 2005)*

How's that for planning? And don't forget the special clothing that some of these activities will need – and new equipment, and even new foods for sustenance. Go on, go for broke. Except it's us that'll go broke.

Dammit. That's got me thinking about the Olympics. Sorry, I need another quote or two, and we'll have to go back to Labour's Manifesto. But first let's take a break; I've got a little quiz:

Who said this?   'The School itself must set aside infinitely more time for physical conditioning. Not a day should pass in which the young person's body is not schooled at least an hour every morning and evening, and this in every sort of sports and gymnastics.'

And this?   'The integral functions of sport are great. This has immense importance for our multinational State. Sports contests and various types of sporting competition have played an important part in cementing the friendships of our peoples.'

And this?   'Every child should have a minimum of two hours
                       compulsory Physical Education a week within the
                       school curriculum . . . Youth sport provides the
                       foundation of sporting excellence.'

The answers are respectively Adolf Hitler (our environmentalist of the
Third Reich), Nikita Krushchev and Sport England.

Now to that manifesto:

> Investment in school sports will ensure that by 2010 all children will
> receive two hours high quality PE or sport per week.
>
> *(Labour Party Election Manifesto 2005)*

Yes, not very different is it? Of course, the Manifesto also refers to an
Olympic Legacy (what else?) to which, despite enormous 'mission
creep' already (see Chapter 6), all the politicos sign up.

Even though I like sport, I don't see why people who don't should
pay – for a legacy which will almost certainly be a white elephant.
Olympic legacies nearly always are.

But that's democracy for you. Two wolves and a lamb voting on
what to have for lunch. Freedom!

As an Italian immigrant in Chicago wrote home to his parents in
the 1930s, 'I remember we voted in Italia and things always got worse
instead of better. What makes America great is not our right to vote,
but the rights we have that protect us from those for whom we vote.'[4]

Sadly, no longer. And this chapter is already long enough.

Appendix: Profit–loss calculation

The enormous advantage of private 'for-profit' organizations is that meaningful
profit–loss calculations can be made, via the phenomenon of double-entry bookkeeping. According to Goethe in 1795–6, double-entry bookkeeping was 'one of
the finest inventions of the human mind'. Bearing in mind the voluntary nature
of private enterprise activities throughout the whole process, from funding to
delivery, with every transaction leaving every participant better off, a profit[5] is an

---

4 *The Market Economy; A Reader*, James Doti and Dwight Lee, Roxbury Publishing Company, Los Angeles, 1991.

5 True profit is calculated after allowing for the going rate of (risk-free) interest.

increase in society's wealth, signalling the efficient allocation of a myriad of resources, whilst a loss is a reduction in society's wealth, signalling the opposite.

Outside private enterprise, the system of profit–loss accounting is quite simply unavailable. Double entry book keeping itself permits the tracking and reconciliation of income and expenditure, so one can understand why the European Union, with funds being moved around and spent without trace, doesn't use it, and why its 'accounts' have not been signed off for at least 12 years. More than 200 years after Goethe, the UK government is at last getting round to it, although even now the accounts of several major departments such as the Home Office are so chaotic that they cannot be signed off by the Auditor General.

In any case, correctly totted up expenses in the public sector cannot be confronted by income equivalents; there are no sales proceeds and the only income comes from donations in one form or another. If this income is spent then the only solution is to ask the donors (which include government, having milked the taxpayers) for more or to go bust.

Without sales proceeds from voluntary purchases, there can be no economic testing and that means chaos. That is why Nikita Krushchev said 'When all the world is communist, Switzerland will have to remain capitalist so that it can tell us the price of everything.' But that was not enough; even a *shortage* of relevant external prices will not save a monolithic organization. The tipping point, where the savings created by a merger are outweighed by the resulting scarcity of relevant market prices, represents the maximum possible size for a private business firm. Beyond that there is increasing inefficiency.

If the NHS, the third largest employer in the world (yes the other two are government-owned as well) were sold to private enterprise, it would be split off into many entirely separate companies. As it is, bureaucracy, i.e. hundreds of rules and targets, is the only way of keeping any kind of tabs at all, inferior tabs though they are. One such tab is the internal use of 'tariffs', i.e. prices, for hospital operations. These prices come from – guess where? Yes, private hospitals, the equivalent of Krushchev's Switzerland.

Leaving the NHS, state education and state welfare to the professionals and their trade unions will simply not do, David Cameron (see Chapter 3). Yes, the NHS ran tolerably well for its first decade or so because it left its old procedures intact, but as they became less and less relevant there were no rational means of deciding on how the NHS should be run. Now, to all intents and purposes, it is broken.

9

One Rule for Them Crap

The rule of law, in complex times,
Has proved itself deficient.
We much prefer the rule of men.
It's vastly more efficient . . .

So, nutshell-wise, the way it is,
The law is what we say it is!
                (From The Incredible Bread Machine *by R. W. Grant)*

The essence of the rule of law is that in both benefits and obligations it applies equally to all people (them as well as us), and that it must have existed as a general rule before any case to which it is applied. Which is precisely why the Constitutional Reform Act (2005) refers to it, but doesn't define it!

No doubt John Reid thinks it's something to do with 'Law and Order' as interpreted by him, where he rules the law and his police force creates the order – in other words, the rule of men, or arbitrary decisions made by Authority. Hazel Blears won't mind as long as some of these men are women and are selected by something that passes for a voting system, and of course Tony Blair positively revels in it. This chapter provides examples of the rule of men, applied naturally so as to favour the politicos.

A big story towards the end of 2006 concerned the investigation by the Serious Fraud Office (SFO) into the activities of BAE systems (the largest European arms manufacturer) in five countries – activities which, it is alleged, involved the bribery of officials in these countries in order to gain contracts. One of these countries is Saudi Arabia, which is in line to buy 72 Eurofighter jets from BAE. *This* deal cannot be jeopardized, now can it?

Our relationship with Saudi Arabia is
vitally important for our country.
(Tony Blair, The Times, 16 December 2006)

Would the SFO protest? Not in
public anyway.

It has been necessary to balance the need to maintain the rule of
law against the wider public interest.

(Lord Goldsmith, Attorney-General, House of Commons,
13 December 2006)

As Oliver Kamm put it in *The Times* of 16 December 2006: 'Britain:
the new banana republic'.

Mind you, this bribery business itself seems a bit dodgy. Let's say
you are given a free copy of this book (much better than a ticket to
Wembley or the theatre!) by a businessman anxious for your custom.
If both of you run self-employed businesses, then there's no problem.
Just the same as you paying a lower price for whatever it is you buy.
Who cares? (Maybe Flash Gordon but it has to be morally right to
deprive him of as much money as you can!)

If on the other hand you both have principals e.g. a Chief Executive
and your company's shareholders, then you are accountable to them
for your actions – but again nobody else.

If BAE payments to foreign officials are approved by its principals
then *the only possible crime is committed by the foreign officials*, who
have defrauded *their* government and more importantly its tax payers.
(I hold no particular brief for BAE, which, because its main customers are governments, cannot be classified as practising free enterprise – see Chapter 10. But that is not relevant here.)

But the Rule of Men says 'government is always blameless – and acquisitive'. Hence the 'bribery' of overseas officials was made illegal in the UK in 2002, allowing yet more expansion of government (via prosecutions and fines under the new law).

Steve Wilmott is the head of 'economic crime' (you have to call it something!) at City of London Police and, recently backed by the Government to the tune of another £3 millions, he's onto some 'ten top UK businesses' (quite independent of the BAE case):

> 'The allegations are simple – that a UK company has bribed a foreign official to take a contract,' said Wilmott. 'The companies are all well-known. The bribes are all for fairly large sums of money . . . we're talking hundreds of thousands plus.'
>
> *(Steve Wilmott, reported in the* Daily Telegraph, *22 October 2006)*

More lolly for government. The more you investigate 'bribery' of this kind, the more you realize it's another government racket. Tell you what, Steve. Why don't you have a look at the leaked report on serious corruption in the Met, reported in the *Sunday Telegraph* of 11 February 2007? Or if that's too close to home, at the 700 corruption cases levelled *in one year* against Home Office immigration staff (as found by a Parliamentary Committee in July 2006)? Might we be talking also of 'hundreds of thousands plus', in each case? One rule for them.

Just like the 'loans for ermine scandal' in which political parties break or severely stretch the rules of engagement. Yet Lord Falconer sees no wrong:

> I don't hold the view that making a donation to a political party in which you believe debars you from any honour.
>
> *(Lord Falconer, Lord Chancellor, reported in* The Times, *11 March 2006)*

Except that if the two are related it's against the law. (None of your mob would even sail close to the wind, would they? What a preposterous suggestion.) Bit dodgy in any case, though – the 'honour' comes from a *governing* party on behalf of we the sheeple – a party which will get kicked out long before you do (being a Lord and all that guff).

By the summer Lord Levy wants to rob us the people instead; he 'is understood to have told MPs to have been converted to the idea of State funding after the controversy surrounding his cash-raising exploits', said *The Times* of 23 June 2006. And by February 2007 Sir Hayden Philips's review is actively considering taxpayer funding of £28 millions. They sin, we chip in.

Flash Gordon Brown is keeping mum. He has to protect that famous 'inherited moral compass' that he keeps banging on about. No doubt I'm so old-fashioned to enquire about arms these days. So cocksure is he that he can leave a colleague to tell us about Gordo's vow to replace the Trident 'deterrent':

> Protecting national security is the first duty of any government, and this responsibility will be safe in Gordon Brown's hands.
>
> *(Paul Murphy, Chairman, Parliamentary Intelligence & Security Committee, reported in* The Times, *22 June 2006)*

Any government, Paul? *Any* government? So are you going to propose that all governments join the nuclear club? No, you're going to keep the club for last time's winners and let winners make the rules. We have 'deterrents', others have 'weapons'.

No doubt Brown himself was keeping the lid on publicity about his relationship with Blair – he certainly had his work cut out at his party conference when Cherie Blair said 'that's a lie' to an especially effusive bit of his speech – effusive for Gordon anyway. And just prior to that he told Parliament (14 September 2006) 'Friendships have ups and downs', which prompted Ann Treneman to write in *The Times* the next day 'Yes Gordon, but not bungee jumps'.

Libby Purves plays all this down:

> Blair v Brown, fascinating as it is, is not a substantial conflict, any more than the rows we used to have in my convent school about which Beatle to fancy.
>
> *(Libby Purves,* The Times, *12 September 2006)*

Maybe not substantial for you, Libby (after all, you're a sort of philosopher aren't you?). And perhaps not even for the rest of us. Except, Libby, that it is substantial for *them* – the top two in the UK government for nearly a decade. So what do you philosophize from that?

I'm sure Libby and I can agree on what's really important – crime, for example, especially 'war and terror' where our Tony said after the raid by 250 policemen on a home in Forest Gate in June 2006 – in which two men were arrested (and one of them shot) on suspicion of plotting terrorism, and were discharged a week later:

> I also stand 101 per cent behind the police and the security services . . .
>
> *(Tony Blair, House of Commons, 14 June 2006)*

To which one of the men said: 'He may say he's 101 per cent behind the police but I'm 101 per cent against the bullet that went into my chest.'

Peter Clarke, Head of Scotland Yard's Anti-Terrorist Branch said:

> The point of the raid was to 'prove or disprove' the intelligence that prompted it. That intelligence pointed to a specific and imminent threat to the UK, he said. It may yet prove to have been flawed. Likewise, the shooting of the 23-year-old suspect subsequently arrested in hospital may yet be deemed unnecessary. But these are secondary issues. Given the intelligence available it would have been unforgivable not to order the raid.
>
> *(Peter Clarke, reported in* The Times, *3 June 2006)*

So the raid 'disproved' the intelligence. Is the intelligence going to get better – perhaps by trying to build up some genuine informers, rather than suspecting every Muslim of every crime?

Just before the killing of Jean Charles de Menezes by the police (at a London tube station in July 2005) our top policeman had this to say:

> [Scotland Yard is] the gold standard across the world for dealing with terrorism.

Twenty-four hours later he trumpeted:

> The Met is playing out of its socks.
>
> *(Sir Ian Blair, Commissioner, Metropolitan Police,*
> *both reported in the* Financial Times, *18 July 2006)*

That episode was a catalogue of police errors as most reports, including that of the *Financial Times*, showed. Yet the de Menezes family legal action was defeated and the only other charge was made under Health and Safety legislation. Whitewash or what?

We shouldn't be surprised that 250 policemen can enter your property on the flimsiest of evidence. So can tax inspectors, TV licence agents, and even the RSPCA. What we must all learn to understand is that *your property does not belong to you*. It belongs to *them*. So they have now given themselves the power to take over empty property from those who inherit it, but haven't occupied it or otherwise used or disposed of it for six months after the death of the previous owner:

> Yvette Cooper, the housing and planning minister, said, however, that it was an outrage that empty properties were not being used to tackle housing shortages.
>
> 'There are all kinds of safeguards for owners who leave properties empty through no fault of their own,' she said.
>
> 'But local councils should be able to take action to deal with the outrage of properties which are abandoned and ignored but blight local communities and deny people needed housing for their area.'
>
> *(Yvette Cooper, Housing and Planning Minister, reported in the Daily Telegraph, 18 June 2006)*

An outrage, eh, Coops? How about the 400,000 empty council houses as opposed to 280,000 private homes (whoops, Coops)? How about MPs' second homes, Dorneywood, and other grace and favour piles for the political class? And just have a little think of what might be causing the housing shortage (see Chapter 8).

Here's another outrage:

> Restaurants and shops should 'grow up' and let the public use their lavatories, Phil Woolas, the Local Government Minister, said.
>
> Mr Woolas was announcing a government strategy this week to shift responsibility for public conveniences to the private sector.
>
> *(Reported in The Times, 21 July 2006)*

Novel! Perhaps the House of Commons will rally round as well?

Oh, no. *Your* lot won't suffer. It's interesting, although galling, to look at Government as a business (yes it takes imagination I know). Pensions are an obvious example where the politicos and the public sector as a whole are in a different league. We all know about their gold-plated benefit formulae, retirement ages, rules and guarantees – or at least we know that they exist. Few readers will know of their sheer magnitude. For example I estimate that Flash Gordon's 1997 tax changes to company schemes puts them out of pocket by well over £100 billion in today's money – and so is responsible for all and more of company schemes' deficits. The tax went to Gordo. The deficits of public sector schemes total about £1000 billion but so what? – taxes on the next generation will pay. Bet you didn't know that the pension of a policewoman adds about 75 per cent to career pay. Doctors' pay increases mean that pensions will be about 40 per cent higher than expected in 2003. 'Civil Servants', not always civil or servile, will go on strike at any attempt to make them pay more. Indeed, university lecturers (with the honourable exception of Buckingham University, the only fully private university in the UK) went on strike in 2006, refusing to mark exam papers, over a 20 per cent pay claim. Public Sector pay is over £60 per week ahead of the private sector *ignoring* pensions. On it goes.

But as soon as we the sheeple come into the picture, it's different. Take state pensions (a silly idea in the first place, but it's there and a big chunk of many people's retirement incomes, although not for the politicos). The retrospective removal of the earnings link means that today's Basic State Pension is around 25 per cent less, relative to average earnings, than it was in 1950. (Various other retrospective reductions have been made to state pensions, especially for widows).

In that light, what do you think of John Hutton?

> I believe that it can lay the foundation for a new and lasting consensus on a long-term solution of the pensions challenge that we face as a country. I commend the White Paper to the House.

> Philip Hammond:
> It is bad news, too, that a degree of uncertainty has now been inserted into the equation by the Chancellor's insistence on the caveat that the restoration of the earnings link in 2012 is subject to some subjective tests of affordability . . .

John Hutton:
However, an important part of that has to be a grown-up approach to affordability issues.

(House of Commons, 25 May 2006)

And there's only one way to be grown up about this; the earnings link *will not be restored* – in 2012 (why are we waiting till then, Gordo?) or at any other time.

Let's look at the land of the free for an interesting ruling:

Dependent on politicians: 'The single most important problem with the current Social Security system is that workers have no ownership of their benefits. The U.S. Supreme Court has ruled, in the case of Flemming v. Nestor, that workers have no legally binding contractual or property right to their Social Security benefits, and those benefits can be changed, cut, or even taken away at any time. This means that workers are completely dependent on the goodwill of 535 politicians when it comes to what they'll receive in retirement.'

(Reported by Michael D. Tanner, Cato@Liberty, 14 August 2006)

How reassuring. That's a nice summary of the position in the UK too – a position which has been illustrated on many occasions.

Nor is there any shame over Iraq: here's GWB in fine voice:

I define success or failure as whether or not the Iraqis will be able to defend themselves. I define success or failure as whether schools are being built or hospitals are being opened.

(George W Bush, Reported in The Times, *20 October 2006)*

On the ground it's a little different:

In the chaos of Iraq, one project is on target: a giant US embassy.

(Reported in The Times, *3 May 2006)*

With 100-odd acres, a swimming pool, and space for over 1,000 residents.

Still think the politicos care? Well they do have their favourites. You can't go treating the BBC like an ordinary business can you?

'One of the questions I think we need to interrogate is the extent to which the costs of other broadcasters are led by the costs of the BBC,' she said. Pressed by peers as to whether pay was part of the market that could be skewed by BBC costs, she said: 'Of course it is', but she stressed that it was 'categorically not for me to set BBC salaries'.

(Tessa Jowell, reported in The Times, *21 April 2006)*

After a long spell of interrogating questions I found that the BBC is exempt from the company regulations concerning directors' remuneration; however it chooses to reveal the figures for certain directors – but NOT for the top earners! When some of the earnings of those top earners were 'leaked' (like Terry Wogan, £800,000) the 'leaker' was called a 'salary mole' in *The Times* (17 May 2006). In the private sector such a person (whose earnings would normally be revealed anyway) would be called a 'whistleblower' or 'a public servant'. In 'public service', he's a 'salary mole' – or a 'snitch' and, as happened here, duly dismissed! Yes, dismissed.

Again, in the private sector, we wouldn't have a CEO bleating to shareholders *and non-shareholders* if they refused to put up money for expansion plans, aka boondoggles, as BBC chief Mark Thomson bleated to Government, aka taxpayers, in January 2007. (And unlike the BBC, and for that matter lots of other government agencies such as the Passport Agency and even the emergency lines of the Metropolitan Police, we'd be hounded by the Office of Fair Trading for using 'rip-off' 0870 telephone numbers.)

How about this for a leak from Health Minister Lord Warner, talking to the House of Lords:

He added that the Government had introduced the reporting system under the NPSA, and the 'leaked document . . . demonstrated that there is a more open culture in the NHS'.

(Lord Warner, House of Lords, 14 July 2006)

An open leak! Only trouble was that the leak came after eight months from receipt of the relevant report from the Mental Health Observatory. This report detailed more than one hundred cases of sexual assault and harassment in less than two years – including nineteen rapes.

It gets comical in the end, doesn't it? It's no surprise to find that the 'Palace of Westminster' including the House of Commons is exempt from the smoking ban due in July 2007 in all public places and work places – and from licensing laws as well.

As we have seen with the BBC example, you're guilty in any case if you work for the State and you upset them. You can be dismissed, court-martialled and jailed if you refuse to serve in Iraq under conscientious objection even if you've done two years there already [Dr Malcolm Kendall-Smith]. You can be hounded to death if you can't find the right evidence of weapons you're asked to seek – and the hounders get promoted [David Kelly]. You can be arrested and fined for wearing a 'Bollocks to Blair' tee-shirt [several, including Leicester trader Tony Wright and Charlotte Denis at a game fair] or for heckling at a party conference when you're 82 years old [Walter Wolfgang]. You can be prosecuted for reading out a list of deaths in Iraq if you're within half a mile of Parliament [Maya Anne Evans].

If you haven't yet been convinced of the prevalence of One Rule for the Politicos, another for us the sheeple, then it's worth having a look at a couple of examples from the European Union.

Here's the EU Competition Commissioner:

> No company is above the law. Each and every company, large or small, operating in the European Union must obey EU law, including Competition Law, to the benefit of all companies and European consumers.
>
> *(Ms Neelie Kroes, European Commissioner for Competition, 12 July 2006, imposing a fine of 280m Euros on Microsoft)*

Unless you're a company of government bureaucrats, that is. Then, you don't have to obey any laws about basic accounting (see appendix to Chapter 8). Oh, there aren't any, are there?

And the EU is snobbish about who can join it, with a long list of demands as the price of the accession for Bulgaria and Romania:

> The commission report stated: 'The legislative framework for the fight against corruption has been improved . . . however, there have been few concrete examples of investigations or prosecution or charges of high-level corruption.'

> There had been 'no successful prosecutions for money laundering'
> and there was 'no systemic confiscation of assets of criminals'.
>
> *(Reported by David Charter,* The Times, *27 September 2006)*

They could have found plenty of corruption within the EU *excluding*
Bulgaria and Romania, simply by concentrating on the politicos.

Or they could have looked at the United Nations:

> The UN is guilty of 'corrosive corruption', according to a long-
> awaited investigation published today into the handling of the
> multimillion-pound Iraq oil-for-food programme.
>
> The 1,000-page report by Paul Volcker, former head of the US
> Federal Reserve, found 'serious instances of illicit, unethical and
> corrupt behaviour within the United Nations'.
>
> *(Reported in the* Guardian, *7 September 2005)*

How was this report received a few months later by the new Chief of
Staff at the UN?

> 'The prevailing practice of seeking to use the UN almost by stealth
> as a diplomatic tool while failing to stand up for it against its
> domestic critics is simply not sustainable,' Mr. Malloch Brown said.
> 'You will lose the UN one way or another,' he added.
>
> *(Reported in* The Times, *9 June 2006)*

That's the United Nations, what Stefan Halper, a former White
House and State Department Official, calls a 'miasma' of corruption.

This is where we came in. Time for me to clock out under the EU
Working Time Directive. But first a bit of One Rule for Them on a
global, and even stellar, scale.

From the USA of course:

> We hail the actions of President Bush and the Republican Congress to
> ensure that our nation's efforts to meet our global security commit-
> ments and protect Americans are not impaired by the potential for
> investigations, inquiry, or prosecution by the International Criminal
> Court, whose jurisdiction we do not accept as extending to Americans.
>
> *(US Republican Party Platform, 2004)*

I have a sneaky bit of sympathy in a way – international groups of national governments are so damned corrupt, aren't they?

But then national governments are no better:

> Space: no longer the final frontier but the 51st state of the United States. The new National Space Policy that President Bush has signed is comically proprietory in tone about the US's right to control access to the rest of the solar system.
>
> *(Reported in* The Times, *19 October 2006)*

A pre-emptive strike at private property, despite all that Republican Platform guff about 'The core of ownership in America has always been ownership of private property that a citizen can call his or her own. Republicans respect this tradition.' Yeah, right.

Not so much clocking out as knocked out!

10

Fashionable Crap

You're gouging on your prices
If you charge more than the rest
But it's unfair competition
If you think you can charge less!

A second point that we would make,
To help avoid confusion:
Don't try to charge the same amount
For that would be collusion.

(From The Incredible Bread Machine *by R.W. Grant)*

What is a fashion and how long does it last? For this chapter anyway, a fashion is a widely held belief or practice with no inherent virtue, which has attracted the politicos. As for duration, we're usually looking at years rather than weeks or months – possibly even decades.

What attracts the politicos? In a word, power, its retention and whatever brings it – votes, vested interests and fear. Money comes in handy, while truth holds no special attraction. (The greater the power, the greater the attraction to those on the make and the greater the corruption.[1])

The new kid on the block here is environmentalism, which will have a long shelf-life. The staying power of the urge to lock up non-conformists is proven, fermented by the ignorance of bigots – as well as the job-preservation requirements of hordes of law-enforcers and their advisers. The same goes for use of misleading military terminology like 'war on drugs' and 'price wars'. At the other extreme, fashions in education and health policy can be quite short, with changes driven

---

1 See Chapter 10, 'Why the worst get on top', of F.A. Hayek's *The Road to Serfdom*, Routledge 2001.

by money and revolving doors. In between are 'consumer-protection' and various politically correct 'isms'.

This chapter is a rather eclectic tour, stopping briefly at several of these fashions.

Let's start with crime, be it real or imaginary. In Chapter 2 I referred to John (Bull) Reid's propensity to bang people up and contrasted it with the Rehabilitation of Offenders Act of 1974 which allowed certain convicted criminals to say (later) that they had never had a criminal conviction!

Perhaps not such a bad idea, since then, as now, much 'crime' consisted of actions amongst freely consenting adults and had no victims:

> Sentencing Mr. Silver, of Wilton House, Knightsbridge, Lord Justice Geoffrey Lane said: 'The properties actually owned by you may have been small in number but for years now you have been responsible for running a highly profitable business based on vice and on the capacity of prostitutes in Soho to earn large sums of money, and upon their ability to pay exorbitant rents for flats of which you and your fellow conspirators were owners.
>
> The profits you reaped were enormous and it is quite clear you are a very wealthy man as a result of these activities.'
>
> (Guardian, *20 December 1974*)

My reaction in the first edition was 'Is a man sentenced to six years in prison for running a "highly profitable business" and for becoming a wealthy man? The Judge went on to say that the only mitigating factor was that there was no suggestion that he had ever forced a girl into prostitution. But if he didn't, what sort of a crime had he committed?'

The Prohibition era is still with us. It is good to know that at least some of the UK judiciary is protesting not only against the suspension of habeas corpus (in order to enforce 'freedom' in other parts of the world!) but also against 'the war on drugs'. The Times of 8 August 2006 reported that in Oxford a judge had refused to impose an anti-social behaviour order on a man cultivating cannabis:

> Judge Harris said: 'If you are Sherlock Holmes and you go back to Baker Street and inject yourself with cocaine, as he did, you cannot be called a nuisance. So quietly smoking cannabis at home, not that

it is to be encouraged, I'm not sure at all it constitutes a nuisance. If you are simply growing it, it's no more offensive to neighbours than tomato plants.' He also told Oxford City Council, who applied for the ASBO, that it was 'the sort of thing they do in Russia or China'.

Good on yer, yer honour. But the judiciary can only do so much:

> Devious barristers and ignorant judges are frustrating the Government's attempt to stop details of a woman's sexual past being disclosed in rape trials, according to a report published yesterday . . .
>
> Reforms introduced six years ago under section 41 of the Youth Justice and Criminal Evidence Act were intended to prevent evidence of past behaviour being put before a jury in England and Wales unless it was relevant to the case. But researchers said the rules were frequently "evaded, circumvented and resisted".
>
> *(From a Home Office-commissioned study of rape trials, published on 20 June 2006)*

So John Bull's Home Office *doesn't want* previous history to be disclosed, a stance 100 per cent (or is it 101, Tony?) opposed to its position on virtually everything else it can influence in this field, from sex-offenders to would-be Santa Clauses.

In rape cases, there is rarely a proof – just claim and counter-claim, yet the defendant cannot call up the claimant's track record. Good luck to the devious barristers, I say.

But I'm wrong, says *The Times*:

> Last year the defendant in a Swansea rape trial was acquitted because the prosecution admitted it could not prove that the alleged victim had withheld her consent for sex. She had been drunk, and the judge directed the jury to return a verdict of not guilty. If this were an isolated case it would be, at best, unfortunate for all concerned; at worst, a grave miscarriage of justice. But it is not isolated. Barely 5 per cent of rape allegations result in convictions.
>
> *(The Times, leading article, 30 March 2006)*

Can you believe this? Yes, in a lot of rape cases, a rapist is getting away with it. The answer, says *The Times*, is to bag a higher proportion and if a few hundred innocents are convicted, what the hell? It's the numbers that count. In which case, it'd be a lot cheaper to draw lots. First five hundred picked out of the bag, down you go. (Also *The Times* is misleading here; the conviction rate is 50 per cent, not 5 per cent, of cases that actually reach the courts.)

The illiberal bent of nearly all today's politicians is manifest in all kinds of fashions. Smoking, for example, crops up on both sides of the Atlantic. I'm not a smoker myself and I will walk out of a restaurant or a pub on those grounds. But as with so many things, the peaceful solution centres on private property. I have read countless articles on the smoking issue which simply ignore (or are ignorant about) private property. Thus the BBC News website announcing that in England the ban will start on 1 July 2007 said this:

> The ban covers virtually all enclosed public places including offices, factories, pubs and bars, but not outdoors or in private homes.
>
> *(Reported by news.bbc.co.uk, 1 December 2006)*

To my no doubt simple mind, offices, factories, pubs and bars are not 'public places'. Like homes, they are *private* places with conditions of entry set by their owners – many of whom have been operating an anti-smoking policy for several years. Many others have not. What could be simpler?

Does that principle operate in the land of the free? No, sirree, although if you smoke in casinos in New Jersey you're laughing:

> This past January acting New Jersey Governor Richard J. Codey signed into law a *state-wide smoking ban* in 'public' places except for casinos. ABC News's Nightline recently aired a segment on this legislation which is set to go into effect on April 15 . . .
>
> Chicago joins them Monday, when a ban on smoking in public places goes into effect, but the law gives taverns and restaurant bars in the city until 2008 to comply.
>
> New Jersey exempted gambling areas at the request of Atlantic City's $5 billion-a-year casino industry, which said a total smoking ban would cause losses in profits, state tax revenues and jobs.
>
> *(Reported by Fox News.Com/world/national, 15 January 2006)*

Casinos, eh? Powerful institutions, US casinos, at least the non-internet variety, which have managed to outlaw online betting via intensive lobbying – and to arrest the chief executives of two British internet gambling firms. Gets more and more like the *old* Prohibition every day.

No surprise there, I suppose. After all, the Republican Party *was formed* to intervene in business and strike cosy deals.

In a word, what we have here is corporatism, a mix of big government and big business. Another unholy alliance – making the prime requirement of a big businessman that of a lobbyist rather than an entrepreneur. In case you hadn't noticed, I am a fan of free enterprise – it's voluntary and peaceful (and anti-war) and it works; I am *emphatically not a fan of big business* except in the very unusual circumstances (today) when it also practises free enterprise. *And contract work for government is never free enterprise.* Here's an example, from some of those who would benefit from ID cards, in the shape of a letter to the Tories:

> I have read with concern your pledge that an incoming Conservative government would cancel the ID card scheme . . .
>
> It is wholly inappropriate for the industry to be used as a mechanism for scoring political points.
>
> *(John Higgins, Director-General of Intellect, The Times, 10 February 2007)*

Intellect is 'the trade association for the UK hi-tech industry'. Free-wheeling entrepreneurs? Yeah right.

Under corporatism, consumers and shareholders don't count for much. There is even a book called *The Big Ripoff: How Big Business and Big Government Steal Your Money.*[2]

Most big businesses love and promote this climate. A fine UK example is National Grid, whose new Chief Executive, Steve Holliday, told the *Sunday Telegraph* on 7 January 2007, 'I love the fact we have seven regulators'. Edison must be turning in his grave.

Protecting your business by regulation (often crafted by you!) and licensing[3] is far easier than having constant pesky battles against com-

2 Timothy Carney, Laissez-Faire Books, Arkansas, USA (http://LFB.com).

3 In many cities in the USA a taxi can set you back around half a million dollars.

petition and potential competition. Especially when consumers, in particular self-styled consumer groups with lobbying power, join in the fun as they usually do, routinely removing the consumer's best friend, competition – in quality and trust as well as price – from the scene.

The Competition Commission allegedly promotes competition but in fact does nothing of the sort; it paralyses it by outlawing 'predatory' pricing (under its own definitions) which, contrary to its own gospel, is often the best way in for small fry – see Chapter 12. When markets are allowed, competition also takes place in the provision of useful information.

So can we have competitive, market-led regulations to help consumers? No, that would be far too sensible and *unfashionable*. Like Gordo's 'only the state can guarantee fairness', only the state can regulate. Here is Matthew Syed, the sports writer and budding politico who favours the oxymoron of government science (see Chapter 7). This time he's mad with Tesco which, like Wal-Mart, has been (so far) a pretty staunch defender of free enterprise.[4] It has also had the temerity to compete with the politicos on a food labelling system. But that's hallowed turf, hollers Matthew:

> Tesco's refusal to adopt 'traffic light' labelling is a recipe for disaster. The retail giant has trampled on proposals for front-of-pack, colour-coded information on the levels of sugar, saturates, salt and fat, the over-consumption of which is placing intolerable strains on the NHS.
>
> *(Matthew Syed, The Times, 10 April 2006)*

There's *no* labels like *state* labels, there's *no* labels I know . . . (catchy little number, that).

In fact Tesco believes that its own labelling system is better than the politicos' offering, and is prepared to let its customers choose. Customers? Choose? Silly me.

Now we're getting to the nitty gritty: the 'intolerable strains on the NHS'. This fashionable refrain is a hallmark of politicos of every hue. Is that why the NHS doesn't label its own food, Matthew, which in my experience defies description?

---

4 Subject only to the vagaries of Stalinist planning permission from the politicos.

We're really into Health Socialism now – Command and Control. Command the tax (whether you use the NHS or not). Control lifestyles according to the latest fashion for what is and isn't healthy – food, drink, exercise, you name it, and use Health Police as necessary. We can go to hell under your fashion, not ours.

Sorry to go on, Matthew, but I have one more question. If you don't think consumers can suss out food labels, despite every incentive to do so, how do you think we'll get on with sussing out the politicos and going to the ballot box (when we have better ways of spending our time and there's not a cat in hell's chance of our own individual vote making a ha'p'orth of difference)? How about a health warning on voting slips – 'Voting can make you sick'?

If you think this is a bit strong, try this:

> Edward Atkinson, a 75-year-old anti-abortion activist, was jailed recently for 28 days for sending photographs of aborted foetuses to the Queen Elizabeth Hospital in King's Lynn, Norfolk. That draconian sentence was not deemed punishment enough: the hospital has banned Mr Atkinson from receiving the hip replacement operation he was expecting . . .
>
> Ruth May, the hospital's chief executive, claims that the ban is justified because the 'offensive' publications he mailed caused 'great distress' to her and her staff and thus contravened the NHS policy of 'zero tolerance'. Some may already feel that such policies make it seem as if a hospital's priority is to protect its staff against the patients, rather than protecting patients from illness. This case goes farther, equating the posting of offensive photos with punching a nurse on the nose . . .
>
> *(Reported by Mick Hume,* The Times, *12 May 2006)*

Now there's a novel way of rationing. Novel and chilling.

So we're not allowed to eat what food we like; nor are we allowed to decide when and where to buy it. As far as the 'when' is concerned, one refrain is 'never on a Sunday' – at least only in government-determined shops and government-determined hours. The Association of Convenience Stores successfully lobbied to keep the Sunday Trading Act 1994 which restricts 'large shops' to six hours of Sunday opening:

The submission argues that buyer power is becoming ever more concentrated with the Big Four grocers. Far from benefiting the consumer, this trend is undermining choice by threatening the future of independent retailers.

The planning system is an ineffective check on the further dominance of the major supermarkets. National planning policy promoting town centres is vitally important to the sector, and should be made stronger and more efficient.

(ACS Submission to Competition Commission, September 2006)

And they were successful – so not much 'convenience' for shoppers there. The ACS website does refer to its own consumer research showing that a majority prefer the restrictions. But leaving aside the notoriety of misleading polls (to say nothing of the divine right of the majority to persecute the minority), can we assume that these consumers wouldn't change their behaviour if the restrictions were lifted? Or is it a case of 'Do as I say not do as I do'?

Perhaps it is; writing in the *Sunday Telegraph* of 9 July 2006, Mary Wakefield said she was shocked at the casual dishonest shoplifting of her friends, saying 'everybody does it'. A follow-up letter confirmed that everybody also does it with insurance claims, adding 'a few extras' to claims. My own experiences are similar. So all you consumers (*producers* in working hours, of course) who rage about rip-offs, why don't you direct some rage at your fellow-consumers – and buy shares in the rip-off companies to make a killing from their vast profits. (Are supermarkets' profits vast? Well, er, no. Only about 4 per cent of total sales, which looks pretty tight to me. And that's before allowing for any return on capital at all (see Chapter 8). They certainly compete on prices – gouging, of petrol prices or anything else, is the last thing the Competition Commission will be able to find. They'll find a 'price war' instead and call it predation!)

There's yet another way in which the politicos influence where and when we can buy food:

By choosing to buy local food we can cut down on wasteful food miles and carbon emissions . . .

(Peter Ainsworth, Shadow Environment Secretary, Conservative Party Conference 2006)

Food miles, eh? Or Food Patriotism, as your boss David Cameron says. Another protection racket, I say. Tell me Peter, how much does a food-mile cost, and how much does a carbon emission cost – both compared to the loss of efficiency (energy, land and so on?). You have no answer, have you? But we do know that waste, and almost certainly net emissions as well, from the current hydrocarbon economy is very much smaller than it was under the old carbohydrate economy. In particular the increase in forests which absorb CO_2 – an increase which is due to land released in moving from inefficient farming, would slam loudly into reverse under 'food patriotism', destroying much of the developing world to boot.

This is a new fashion, a new religion even, and the Tories are hooked. What a wonderful way to increase taxes, in the name of the planet.

The particular trademark of this religion is that it refuses to consider costs and trade-offs. 'What are trade-offs?' they say. They prefer cuddles and pictures:

> If you want to understand climate change, go and see Al Gore's film, *An Inconvenient Truth* . . .
> That would create a price for carbon in our economy.
> *(David Cameron, Conservative Party Conference 2006)*

Been there, seen that. A Convenient Untruth, I call it. Full of holes, bent hockey stick, 95 per cent political. And as to the price, just give us it, Dave. 1p per unit? £1 million per unit? Is this where Dave the Vague comes in?

By the way, Dave, you know that article of yours 'I'm going to put Britain on a green highway', in the *Daily Telegraph* of 23 April 2006? Did you notice the letter on the same day from forty-one scientists debunking the global warming alert? Bad timing, Dave.

I once read a book which documented some of the trendy schools that taught the environmentalist religion. It was combined with music lessons, so the kids could sing 'this is the way to trash our cans, trash our cans, trash our cans'. You get the drift.

I can't find that book but I'm often reminded of it by the politicos singing hymns to the god of environmentalism. David Miliband's 'The Three Planets' (see Chapter 1) has great potential. So does this one:

The battle against climate change is an economic issue, a social issue, a security issue. It is also a political issue.

(David Miliband, Labour Party Conference 2006)

The Four Climate Issues. Verse I: Economic. Verse II: Social . . .

And so on he goes. He certainly goes; just before the Conference he was in Mexico and the next month in Kenya, emitting god knows what on all sides. And we have since discovered that Ian Pearson, the Climate Change Minister who berated the boss of Ryanair as the unacceptable face of capitalism, flew about 22,500 miles in the past year. True to form, it wasn't long (January 2007) before Miliband attacked the Prince of Wales for flying to New York to collect an environmental award.

Way back at manifesto time in 2005 there was only one issue – the front door:

The environment starts at the front door.
(Labour Party Election Manifesto 2005)

Oh no it doesn't. (Come on, everybody, louder. 'OH NO IT DOESN'T!')

It starts at *all* external doors. *The problems* start at the front door though. The back and side doors show the solution, since they open onto private land not public land. That's why they're cleaner and free of the litter, graffiti, fly-tipping and all those other things mentioned in the 2005 Clean Neighbourhoods and Environment Act. It is also why privately owned communities have nothing like the same problems. Re-privatize the streets. And the roads, where road pricing would be standard. But you can bet your bottom dollar that in government hands it will not only be additional to current taxes but also it will be used for further snooping.

It really starts with YOU, David; government and its acolytes. Thus we have the Sustainable Consumption Roundtable, a 'joint initiative from the National Consumer Council and Sustainable Development Commission, funded wholly by government' (i.e. by *us*). It is charged with 'building wide ownership of sustainable consumption and pro- ducing practical advice to government for actions and policies to create a shift to more sustainable lifestyles'.

Glad to know my money is in good hands, although I'm a bit more interested in sustainable sustenance myself, and I've never seen a gov- ernment sustain anything worth having. There's always a first time.

I'd better stop ranting about the new religion. Uses up too much space when there are important things to do. I'm in danger of getting through a whole chapter without mentioning our National Diseduca- tion Service. (We can only hope that the environmental god is equally flighty with its fashions.)

Here's a Labour Manifesto 'pledge':

> By 2006 every school supported to offer all pupils access to comput- ers at home.
>
> *(Labour Party Election Manifesto 2005)*

Sounds a bit ambitious. Or not? Because 'books are more than twice as effective as computers in raising standards among pupils', says Steve Hurd, a senior academic who spent thirty years training teachers to use computers (reported in the *Daily Telegraph*, 20 May 2006).

Is it possible to believe there's a backlash re dumbing down?

> A-Level exams will be made tougher with a return to traditional questions as part of sweeping reforms to help universities and employers identify the brightest students.
>
> *(Reported in* The Times, *15 July 2006)*

H'm. We'll see. This looks more like it:

> Students are to be allowed to pass GCSEs in science entirely through multiple-choice examinations and coursework.
>
> *(Reported in* The Times, *10 June 2006)*

Meanwhile here's Geoff Hoon, Minister for Europe (at the last check-point):

> Geoff Hoon, the Minister for Europe, has written to Alan Johnson, the Education Secretary, calling for a boost in EU lessons in the national curriculum, The Times has learnt. Mr Hoon said that he was concerned that children were indifferent to the EU because they were not taught about benefits such as free trade and cheap travel . . .
>
> 'I certainly think that that should be part of the national curriculum, a part of the citizenship process.
>
> 'I have no doubt there should be an element in there that explains what the EU is and how it works.'
>
> *(Geoff Hoon, reported in* The Times, *1 August 2006)*

And this?

> PUPILS as young as 14 should learn how to change a nappy, bath a baby and recognise the first signs of meningitis, teachers will be told this week.
>
> Lynn Edwards, the outgoing chairwoman of the Professional Association of Teachers, will call for parenting classes to be made compulsory for all pupils aged 14 to 16.
>
> *(Reported in* The Times, *31 July 2006)*

Poor little kiddies. So much to learn. And we mustn't forget David Lammy's history lessons (see Chapter 8).

But this should provide a bit of breathing space:

> Schools would no longer be required to teach children the difference between right and wrong under plans to revise the core aims of the National Curriculum.
>
> *(Reported in* The Times, *31 July 2006)*

I feel more comfortable with that. There won't be so much crap for parents to debrief. And teachers themselves must be always debriefing something; over the last generation there are scores if not hundreds of U-turns in the annals of state education. Selection, special needs, reading methods, discipline, sex education, exams, Standard Assessment Tasks. Make up your own U-turn list. Even make it into a model railway, full of sharp bends.

The real problem is the idea of a national curriculum in the first place. To anyone who asks 'Should there be sex education (or whatever else is the flavour of the month) in our schools?' another question is in order: 'Should there be pizzas in our restaurants?'

Other 'ISMS' do the rounds too. Multiculturalism is a good example of a situation where simple market solutions, for example private property rights, are never allowed to see the light of day. Take, for example, the row about wearing veils:

> Muslim women should be banned from wearing the veil, to improve security and cohesion in Britain, the Church of England's only Asian bishop has said . . .
>
> 'It is fine if they want to wear the veil in private, but there are occasions in public life when it is inappropriate for them to wear it,' he said . . .
>
> 'Given that we are facing an unprecedented security situation, legislation needs to be introduced that allows officials to remove the veil,' the bishop told *The Sunday Telegraph* . . .
>
> Bishop Nazir-Ali, whose father converted from Islam to Catholicism, said that the legislation should not just cover airports, but should extend to all areas of travel where an identity needs to be established, such as tube and train stations and ports . . .
>
> Laws should also be given to employers and boards of trustees to demand that the veil is not worn at work, he said.
>
> *(The Rt Rev Michael Nazir-Ali, Bishop of Rochester, reported in the* Sunday Telegraph, *24 December 2006)*

Just as with smoking bans, the issue of private versus public property, and of what constitutes the latter, is hopelessly muddled. And the weaselly introduction of 'public life' muddies the waters further. (Or perhaps the proposal concerns only the politicos? Chortle, chortle.)

According to the Bishop, 'public places' include places of employment. I'm sorry to have to tell you, Bishop, that I'm writing this in a place of employment which is a room in my place of residence and if anyone wants to come in wearing a veil, my wife and I will make the decision (well, my wife anyway), which will have nothing whatsoever to do with veils.

Or crucifixes. OK, British Airways made a bit of a fool of itself in banning a crucifix but it learned its lesson, *and applied it*, pretty quickly. Not bad for a company that's as much corporatist as private – as it must be as long as government controls take-off and landing slots.

The idea of 'quotas' in the workplace is an insult to all the nationalities and ethnic groups concerned, whether a majority or otherwise. Until the politicos get to work. Like Lord Warner:

> We need all kinds of doctors in the modern NHS to ensure that we reflect the populations that we serve.
>
> *(Lord Warner, reported in* The Times, *10 March 2006)*

Be nice to think ability would get a look in somewhere. No fear. Similarly, both Harriet Harman and Tessa Jowell think they deserves Prescott's job:

> So Ms Harman has resorted to an indisputable quality to justify her bid for Mr Prescott's job: she is a woman. 'In purely electoral terms, let alone anything else, it would be a miscalculation not to have a woman,' she has said.
>
> A potential rival for the role, Tessa Jowell, also points to her gender as strengthening her candidature. 'I think it is a very good principle that the Government should look like the rest of the country,' she told an interviewer last week.
>
> *(Reported by Patience Wheatcroft,* Sunday Telegraph, *24 September 2006)*

Patience Wheatcroft, the editor of her paper and rightly so, observes that 'Such a view is a very good reason why neither Ms Jowell nor Ms Harman should be promoted to a role which, for some time yet, could see the incumbent left in charge of the country while the leader is on holiday.'

Patience knows that (unlike the political market), the free market is colour blind, sex blind, culture blind, and everything else blind; few businesses would deliberately disadvantage themselves for the sake of a prejudice. They can go bust; governments can't.

My regular paper during the week is *The Times*, which is why I occasionally heap praise on an article and less occasionally don't. It is sad to see one of the most staunch guardians of liberty publishing many illiberal, and sometimes barely literate, articles.

This one's right on the button:

> But what exactly is meant by 'Left' and 'Right' in the post-socialist 21st-century world?
>
> There are three different ways of defining the Left–Right spectrum, roughly corresponding to three different traditions of socialism: Marxist socialism, which demanded state control of the economy and opposed private ownership of the means of production; Fabian socialism, which focused on redistribution of income and wealth from the rich to the poor; and Beveridge or welfare-state socialism, which emphasised state provision of social services. With the benefit of hindsight the Left–Right axes defined by these three traditions can now be seen as quite distinct. What complicates any assessment of how Britain might fare after the Blair–Brown transition is that the Prime Minister and the Chancellor have occupied quite different positions on each of these three axes.
>
> *(Anatole Kaletsky,* The Times, *22 June 2006)*

Kaletsky goes on to clear Brown of all three forms of 'socialism'. But there are also three forms of criticism – at the very least.

First off, as they say, the Right–Left spectrum is not a spectrum (Kaletsky is far from alone in this error). It is a line, and the worst kind of simplification imaginable, since Far Right and Far Left are very similar if not identical (fascism being a form of socialism). Where, for example would Kaletsky put Milton Friedman on a Right/Left line, as a passionate advocate of free markets, de-criminalization of drugs and removal of the draft (compulsory military service)?

Far better is a diamond-shaped figure (opposite), such as that depicting the world's smallest political quiz.

Second, one of the most important of things that really matter is the overall size of taxation, where Brown is one of the most socialist senior politicos in the developed world.

Third, as a matter of history, Marxism was founded (and continued) on the assumption that the state would 'wither away'.

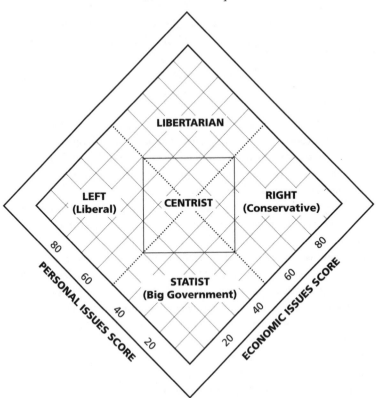

Reprinted with permission, copyright Advocates for Self-government,
www.TheAdvocates.org

On the same day in the same paper we have Political Editor Peter
Riddell twittering on about political democracy (instead of the far
more important market democracy):

> The real need is to strengthen representative democracy by giving
> voters more direct access, and having two-way debates via the
> internet on Bills and select committee inquiries. The public should
> have the right to present petitions that are seriously considered by
> MPs (as already happens in Scotland).
>
> *(Peter Riddell,* The Times, *22 June 2006)*

Peter would love a magic voting machine, by which everybody could vote on any topic at any time (including the existence of his newspaper, I presume). The majority vote (again, I presume) wins and the minority (irrespective of size of majority, strength of feeling, knowledge, or anything else) lose. We're back to two wolves and a lamb, all day and every day.

A *market* democracy features voting for everybody millions of times a day. It's called freedom, in which the magic of millions of market prices are always available for you to vote on any topic you like at any time you like. Anything that suppresses this wonderful instant messaging service is quite simply censorship.

The inevitable outcome of *collective* voting on everything would be the removal of all voluntary trade; you'd have to ask the electorate before you could reach any agreement with anybody.

If you insist on political democracy, Peter, a far better idea would be to use a different method of voting at elections – the 'Strictly Come Dancing' method. Like many other TV competitions, you can vote as many times as you like, but you have to pay each time. There'd be a real incentive to investigate the politicos properly and your knowledge and degree of desire can come into play. And if the payments go to the party you vote for, they might even be able to raise funds without breaking the law.

Yet again, I'm working decidedly unfashionable hours. It's not sustainable without sustenance. So I'm signing off for now, without putting it to a vote. Byee.

11

Economic Crap

As soon as the economic freedom which the market economy grants to its members is removed, all political liberties and bills of rights become humbug.

(*Ludwig von Mises*, Human Action, *1949*)

It would be great to say that economics has not been contaminated by politics. This book is about politics and I've been banging on for long enough. Unfortunately economics *has* been contaminated – from the study of human action to satisfy wants, with particular reference to exchange and the division of labour, to clearly statist issues. Thus the politicos talk about government management of money and interest rates, protectionism, and the 'balance of payments', much with an underlying and incorrect belief that prosperity in one country is possible only at the expense of another.

So economic crap is political crap under a pseudo-economic cloak. Naturally the underlying issues change as do fashions. Below is my summary of the same chapter in the first edition of this book.

That's the lot. Economic and 'social' are not opposites. Consumers determine prices and incomes. Profits are a public service. Price and income controls produce shortages and unemployment. Furthermore they cannot control inflation, and the Price Commission's boasts that it has saved the consumer so many million of pounds are a lot of hooey – surely actionable under the Trade Descriptions Act. Printing money, nothing else, produces price inflation, and also unemployment. Government spending means taxation. Government spending does not reduce unemployment. The multiplier theory is balls. Speculators are our friends. And foreign dumpers are also our friends. And economics is not as hard as it's made out to be!

I stand by all of this, but some of the major issues have changed. Less on inflation, unemployment and printing money (the three of which together should have consigned Keynesian economics to the dustbins of history). More on trade and immigration. Specific rather than general price and income controls. The invention of 'economic crime'. The rise and rise of government and the (not unrelated) virtual disappearance of 'capital' from the language of economics.

Let's start with trade. Free enterprise is inextricably bound up with free trade. The UK doctrine of laissez-faire and free enterprise, within and across borders, was a doctrine of international peace in which the frontiers of nations are immaterial to their citizens. War was common before this doctrine came on the scene and after it went, but not in between (broadly for a generation or two either side of 1850).

Gordon Brown wants us to think he is passionately in favour of free trade across borders (although he is passionately against it within borders – see the introduction to Chapter 7).

On the face of it there's little wrong here:

> I have found a shared view among business that the priority for any advanced economy like ours is: . . .
>
> to be for free trade and open markets . . .
>
> *(Gordon Brown, CBI Annual Conference 2006)*

[My truncation does not distort the whole quotation.]

Nor here:

> Across the world, we are seeing not only the impact of terrorism . . . We also see a surge of protectionism . . . Without a forward momentum a new trade agreement would give, we risk rolling backwards to the age of beggar-thy-neighbour protectionism . . .
>
> *(Gordon Brown, Financial Times, 28 August 2006)*

There are countless remarks of Gordon Brown similar to those above. Most of them *appear to be in favour of free trade* – but to Brown students the tell-tale signs are there. We are 'for' free trade and 'a new trade agreement' and 'against' 'beggar-thy-neighbour'.

Here, Flash Gordon's deception is becoming clear:

We did it before, we'll do it again: my call to the champions of world trade . . .

In the 19th century Britain led the world in equating free trade with liberty only when business and politicians came together for that shared purpose. In this new century the same kind of joint effort is required from government and business before the last window closes to restart the talks.

(Gordon Brown, reported in The Times, *6 November 2006)*

(The 'talks' were *inter-governmental* talks which broke down in Doha in July 2006.) I'm sure you know, Gordo, that the defining feature of the free trade practised by the UK following Robert Peel's Act of 1846 was just that; free trade, *declared unilaterally.* If it is hindered by government 'protectionism' in one country, there is no reason to hinder it in another. But your use of the expression 'beggar-thy-neighbour' shows that you have no understanding of free trade. Protectionism is 'beggar-thy-neighbour-*and-thyself*'.

In fact, Gordon Brown is in favour of *un*free trade. Free trade between two people or businesses always benefits both parties, whether or not a national border is involved. If in some instances one government stops a trade, then that's bad luck but it makes no sense for another government to react by stopping another. That would be making two errors not one.

Yet this is Gordo's position. Needless to say, it's David Cameron's and George Osborne's too.

It's time we had a campaign for Unilateral Free Trade – running alongside a campaign for Unilateral Nuclear Disarmament.

Peter Mandelson, the European Trade Commissioner, puts them to shame:

The core message is rejection of protectionism at home and activism in opening markets abroad. Europe needs to import. It cannot argue for openness from others while sheltering behind barriers of its own.

Oh no he doesn't! From the same speech:

Mr Mandelson rejected suggestions of double standards as he presented his blueprint just hours after EU member governments had agreed to impose anti-dumping duties of up to 16.5 per cent on cheap shoes from China and Vietnam.

'It is very important if we stand up for free trade that we keep in place proper defences against unfair trade,' he said.

(Peter Mandelson, reported in The Times, *5 October 2006)*

Free trade isn't fair, Mandy, without your say so, eh?

The same goes for *The Times* Business Editor, James Harding:

Last year the British bought 12 per cent of their car insurance online. By 2009 this will rise to 29 per cent. Each time they search for a quote, the motorist keys their name and address into a website. That data entry used to be someone's job . . .

In 1991 the insurance and pensions industry employed 250,000 people. By 2004 it was 208,000. Unless drivers abandon their taste for cheap cover and internet convenience, tens of thousands more jobs will disappear overseas and into the digital ether.

(James Harding, The Times, *15 September 2006)*

But lo and behold, all those drivers with their cheaper cover will have more money to save or spend on something else, creating more jobs either way. Come on James, this is in the Harford Thomas class.

And for David Cameron, always on cue, this time at home:

In a speech on Tuesday, his first on the world economy, Mr Cameron said there was a need to be 'honest' about the costs of globalisation.

In yet another break from the tone of his predecessors at the head of the party, he said there were towns in Britain 'where the winds of globalisation feel like a chilling blast, not an invigorating breeze.'

(David Cameron, speaking in India, reported in the Financial Times,
6 September 2006)

You name the towns, Dave, and I'll show you the real causes. Deal, or no deal? (Here's a clue; the Farewell State.)

And I bet you didn't visit any of those private schools for the poor that James Tooley has documented.[1]

Michael Meacher could take a look too. But he's beyond recall; a rich man himself (how many properties do you own, Michael – is it six, by any chance?) singing the praises of council housing whilst he wants to keep the rest of the world in poverty:

> **The poorest countries need tariff walls to protect them from inter-national competition.**
>
> *(Michael Meacher,* The Times, *8 June 2006)*

As a follow-up letter from John Wennstrom to *The Times* argues, Meacher would keep whole continents in hopelessness. As would 'food patriotism' here at home.

The Free Trade issue provides an excellent example of the emptiness of the 'Left versus Right' concept. The Left wing doesn't like foreigners' goods here and the Right wing doesn't like foreigners here!

To go back a little, what explains the change in the cry 'workers of the world unite' to 'workers of the world, don't come here and take away my job'? The short answer is the warfare–welfare state, in which protectionism and interventions of all kinds lead to economic nationalism and war – and restrictions of movement. Much of the anti-immigration feeling in the UK is caused by access to the welfare state, not access to the UK itself. Little more than a century ago, politically controlled freedom of movement wasn't in sight. Now it's all the rage. Even within currently accepted parameters the debate totally ignores

---

1 *Private Schools for the Poor: A Case Study from India*, James Tooley and Pauline Dixon, E G West Centre, Newcastle University, 2003.

two crucial issues – capital and private property. The best we get is a political 'points system' based on work skills.

Actually Australia is a little better than that. If I want to retire in Australia and not do any work at all, I can do so, if I have certain levels of income and assets (and pass certain other tests). Rich immigrants can hardly fail to be a net benefit, whether the riches are brought with them or left behind. One way or another, capital per head is higher and so therefore are living standards.

Of course you can't get everybody into the UK as you could in Australia. (Or the United States, where the Statue of Liberty with its stirring inscription *'Bring me your tired, your poor, your huddled masses yearning to break free . . .'* is totally ignored by George Bush as he orders a 700 mile fence to be built along the Mexican border.)

So in the UK we have problems of space (property) as well as capital.

And those sacred 'Public Services' of course. Dean Godson, once Chief Leader Writer at the *Daily Telegraph* and now Research Director of the think tank Policy Exchange, lauds Migration Watch and its founder Andrew Green, alongside a Professor of Demography and a Professor of Hepatology (representing the NHS as one of the sacred, I presume):

> Thanks to Sir Andrew, it is now socially acceptable to discuss this subject rationally. With much prodding from Migration Watch, it has been officially confirmed that 83 per cent of projected population growth in Britain will come from mass immigration, adding six million people to these islands over 27 years. This will have enormous consequences for public expenditure, for the NHS, for crime – in short, for almost every aspect of state policy. For example, immigration will account for nearly a third of new households, requiring 1.5 million further homes over the next two decades. If this isn't fair game for discussion, what is?
>
> Aided by such leading authorities as David Coleman, Professor of Demography at Oxford University and Professor Roger Williams, director of the Institute of Hepatology at University College London . . .
>
> *(Dean Godson, The Times, 10 June 2006)*

Thanks, Dean. But we're looking in vain for a mention of capital from any of you, including Migration Watch. (Sounds more like *Immigration Watch* to me). Nor do you mention property, as such, which so often provides the key. If there is no such thing as public property and an immigrant or would-be immigrant has valid access to private property (from the owners) then much of the problem disappears. Even without the private property cure-all, massive privatization of government-owned property, together with private sponsorships, would go a long way.

And if the demise of the Welfare State, including nationalized health and education, is hastened then so much the better. Without it there is no problem in the first place!

What about ageing populations and migration? If any body can solve international retirement income problems it ought to be the United Nations. But all we get is a straw man:

> In a clear-headed summary of the great pensions row, the report points out that migration can be only a small part of the answer to the ageing populations of Europe. Migrants may be young when they arrive, but they age, too. Yet no developed country would tolerate the strain of immigration on the vast, sustained scale needed to preserve the age balance.
>
> *(Reported in* The Times, *7 September 2006)*

The report is the UN's annual on the State of World Population. We can forgive the reporter, but the supreme irony in an international body not understanding (clear-headed or not) that the international division of labour allows most 'age-balance' issues to be solved without any migration at all is depressing. Just like Bournemouth or Harrogate, the UK as a whole could be one great big retirement haven, with the retired holding their savings abroad and thus providing higher wages to eager young workers, as well as living off the income. In the UK itself all that would be needed is a few consumer-facing industries like health care and retailing. Always assuming free trade – perhaps that's much too way-out for the UN, despite its name (while unilateral free trade would send the World Trade Organization into apoplexy).

Tell you what, UN, let's have a reports-for-food programme with me writing your reports. After all, oil is a bit old-fashioned these days.

The NHS worshippers still refer to immigrants as 'health tourists'. And believe it or not, the same goes for sick babies:

The Church of England provoked shock yesterday by telling doctors' ethical advisers that some sick babies should be allowed to die.

The Bishop of Southwark, the Right Rev Dr Tom Butler, said that the economic cost of long-term healthcare and education must be considered . . .

'For a Christian, death is not the end, and is not to be avoided at all costs.'

(The Times, *13 November 2006*)

Wasn't this same bishop allegedly found (December 2006) in the back of somebody else's car, throwing out children's toys and saying 'I'm the Bishop of Southwark: that's what I do'? He doesn't like children much does he, sick or otherwise? And with economics like that, clearly he has no time for parents either.

It sounds as if (like Matthew Syed) his God is the NHS, which kills people by law (the sale of organs is illegal). The NHS has a waiting list of 6,000 for kidneys alone. In the land of the free, for similar reasons, *several thousand people die every year* while waiting for organ transplants. The logical end of Big Government is that almost everything is either banned or compulsory, and Health Socialism is leading the way.

Or is it Health Capitalism? The first edition of this book contained numerous examples of the economic illiteracy of Harford Thomas, City Editor of the *Guardian*. This one must take some beating:

They tell me it takes three years to build a brewery. Most of these three years, wages and salaries paid in the building will have been spent before a drop of beer goes on the market . . .

The same timelag reasoning applies to all kinds of expenditures on buildings, factories . . .

Is this not a major cause of inflation because it increases immediate spending demands without any corresponding immediate addition to goods and services?

(Harford Thomas, Guardian, *30 August 1974*)

Inflation was a big issue at the time (and may be so again before too long) but this really takes the biscuit. The very function of a capitalist is to refrain from consuming and to build the factories instead. Spending is not increased; it is *switched*, from consumer goods to capital goods.

Sometimes I wonder if the Principal Economic Commentator and Associate Editor of *The Times* is any better:

> The equilibrium interest rate in a normally functioning economy is roughly equal to the growth rate of GDP.
>
> *(Anatole Kaletsky,* The Times, *12 June 2006)*

This is close to Marxism, where the fundamental error is similar to that of Harford Thomas. A near-universal feature of humanity is that consumption will not be deferred without a reward for waiting. You are hardly likely to lend me a hundred pounds for a few years without a reward for waiting, even if its purchasing power doesn't depreciate. Until scarcity is eliminated, everywhere, waiting always needs a reward. This is called time-preference; a low time-preference means willingness to wait for *little* reward; a high time-preference means a *greater* reward for waiting is required. The same goes for the borrower; borrowing (for immediate consumption) signals a higher time-preference than that of the lender. Like all market transactions and trades, a universal price (i.e. an interest rate in this case) evolves naturally for all identical transactions. Anatole is telling us that the price attached to lending and borrowing transactions is nil unless GDP (a highly dubious and indeed fictitious entity with enormous margins of error) is growing (or shrinking). If you believe this you'll believe anything.

Keynesianism could not survive the concurrence of inflation and recession in the 1970s and is virtually dead for most serious economists. Unfortunately a few dinosaurs (mainly working for government) remain, and Kaletsky (for whom the dinosaurs are 'pre-Keynes') persists in the belief that governments must manipulate money and interest rates to adjust 'demand'. He even defies the chain of UK economic events in the early 1980s, despite being corrected by Sir John Hoskyns, the head of the Prime Minister's Policy Unit at the time.

To Anatole, consumption of beer, and not the building of breweries, is the vital cog:

> The important question for Europe is not whether Germany can keep exporting, but whether the Club Med countries can keep consuming.
>
> *(Anatole Kaletsky,* The Times, *6 March 2006)*

He seems to think that *increasing* consumption of beer, rather than temporarily *reducing* it, will build breweries. No doubt if Robinson Crusoe wanted to build a bigger boat, it would have miraculously appeared if he frenziedly went out fishing in his smaller one every minute of every day!

Interfering with (i.e. censoring) market prices and incomes remains a favourite pastime of politicians. As with Keynesianism, there are few serious economists to be found who support a Minimum Wage Law, which means quite simply compulsory unemployment.

So in many countries of the world, including of course the land of the free where (as in the UK) both major parties support this monstrosity, you have to jump a productivity hurdle before you're allowed to become one of our politicos' avowed favourites, a 'hardworking family'.

One such country is France, of course, with an unemployment rate of at least 10 per cent and no less than 25 per cent for young people. Why? Partly because of the minimum wage, although the government (taxpayers) pay some of that. The bigger reason is the enormously onerous impositions on employers wishing to terminate the employment contract. The infamous riots in Paris (2005/6) arose because of a new law saying that in the case of inexperienced young people, lay-offs in the first two years would be allowed without a specific justification (albeit with compensation).

The rioters won. Free trade, NOT.

But the politicos live in a world of their own. So easily can they make money that they think we're all the same even after they've taken half of ours. So minimum wages and maximum prices are the order of the day. Supply and demand? What's that?

Don't ask a government lawyer:

> My husband and I studied for years to pursue careers in which we would be serving society and in doing so we have incurred huge bank loans. For the next ten years or so, we will struggle to pay

these back, alongside new debts such as mortgages, car loans, the cost of raising children, the odd well-deserved holiday, etc. Hard-working, underpaid people like us are rather aggrieved.

Professionals such as doctors, nurses and teachers are far more crucial to society than any footballer.

(Isabella Abbot, letter to The Times, *30 May 2006)*

As a follow-up letter asked, Isabella, no doubt you work hard, but when did you last have 70,000 people each willing to pay £30 to watch you do it? I'm not a fan of footballers (nor of government lawyers, although I sympathize with you if that wayward Attorney-General, Lord Goldsmith, is your boss) but the only just wage is what people are *willing* to pay. It's called free trade.

Sorry to have found another lady but here's Venus Williams who earned a lot more than most footballers in her heyday:

Wimbledon has sent me a message: I'm only a second-class champion . . . the decision of the All England Lawn Tennis Club yet again to treat women as lesser players than men – undeserving of the same amount of prize money – has a particular sting.

(Venus Williams, The Times, *26 June 2006)*

The irony in this case, Venus is that when you won in 2005 you were paid more than twice as much per game as the men's champion, Roger Federer. That's no more valid than the reasoning of yourself or Isabella of course. But I suggest that both of you read about the role of government price-fixing – (oh yes it's OK when *they* fix prices) and the roles of Big Government and the Farewell State – in the collapse (farewell!) of the Roman Empire.

Perhaps Isabella in particular will be happy that football *followers* have to stump up absurd prices, and not just for tickets:

Retailers are taking advantage of consumers, and parents in particular, by charging almost as much for an England shirt to fit a small child as one that is big enough to fit a 20st (127kg) man.

(Neil Fowler, Editor of Which? magazine, reported in The Times,
1 June 2006)

Or maybe the retailers are being *too generous* to customers, allowing a 20 stone man to pay the same price as a small child. I mean, why should a 20 stone man be allowed to go shopping anyway, when he should be working off his surplus fat to reduce the costs of the NHS?

Censorship of market prices is a favourite activity of politicos around the 'free' world. Oil companies are in trouble in America for more 'economic crime':

> Congressional GOP leaders on Monday formally called on President Bush to launch an investigation into possible price gouging by oil companies, as gas costs shot up nearly 25 cents a gallon in two weeks.
>
> 'Anyone who is trying to take advantage of this situation while American families are forced into making tough choices over whether to fill up their cars or severely cut back their budgets should be investigated and prosecuted,' House Speaker Dennis Hastert, R-Illinois, and Senate Majority Leader Bill Frist, R-Tennessee, wrote in a letter to President Bush. 'Therefore, we believe that Federal law enforcement agencies and regulators should take every available step to ensure that all Federal laws protecting American consumers from price-fixing, collusion, gouging and other anti-competitive practices are vigorously enforced.'
>
> *(Reported by William Anderson, Mises Daily Article, Mises Institute,*
> *26 April 2006)*

I can do no better than quote more of this article in response:

> So, let us trace this sorry story to its most recent beginnings. (1) Congress requires new fuel mixtures during the warm weather months which are costly and disrupt available supplies, but those mixtures do not make the air any cleaner; (2) The President and Congress decide to invade Iraq and now are making threats toward Iran, thus guaranteeing political instability and violence in the largest oil-producing region of the world; (3) Congress requires even more ethanol mixtures, despite the fact that it disrupts supplies and ethanol manufacturers cannot meet the goals; (4) gasoline prices spike, and members of Congress call for arrest and imprisonment of oil executives . . .
>
> There is a way out of this mess – reinstitute free markets in

gasoline and oil – but Congress and the President of the United States, not to mention those who are politically connected, have no intention of permitting the markets to work.

(William Anderson, Mises Daily Article, Mises Institute, 26 April 2006)

Why not call a price-fixing group by its proper name: a cartel?

> Thomas Barnett, who heads the US Department of Justice's antitrust division, told the Financial Times 'the world is becoming less safe for cartel participants. That's a good thing' . . .
>
> Mr Barnett added that global cartels represented the most serious threat to consumers in the world.
>
> *(Thomas Barnett reported in the* Financial Times, *28 July 2006)*

There is really only one genuine concern for the US Anti-Trust Division and the UK Competition Commission, namely monopoly. All their other concoctions are either code-words for monopoly or sheer phooey.

The Appendix to this chapter takes a further look at monopoly, but the fastest way to understand it is to look in Government's own back yard, which provides at a stroke not only the overwhelming examples of harmful monopolistic behaviour but also disproves the conventional cosy theories of private monopolies. Look at the UK's own mammoth industries: the enormous NHS and State Education industries are both 'free', carrying a nil price tag. The ultimate in predatory pricing! Yet the competition is significant and it thrives. Royal Mail, despite its size and infrastructure, has always needed a legal monopoly to survive.

QED.

For Government itself, prices don't exist. Why do all its own operations go wrong?

Peter Riddell thinks he knows:

> The missing element, the elephant in the room that no one mentions, is ministers.
>
> Of course, politics is not the same as business. But some of the failings of the Blair Government are because senior ministers have not understood how big organisations work.
>
> *(Peter Riddell,* The Times, *20 July 2006)*

He's at it again a few days later:

> Ministers are the last remaining untrained amateurs of public life.
> Most arrive in office with no experience of working in large organ-
> isations, let alone of Whitehall.
>
> It is a recipe for misunderstandings, mistakes and mutual suspi-
> cion. But that is about to change: plans are well advanced for the
> formal training of junior ministers . . .
>
> *(The Times, 27 July 2006)*

Perhaps the National School for Government could offer formal help.
I thought that was a spoof, but no such luck:

> The public rightly demands, and should receive, high quality service
> from the Government . . . In the National School of Government, we
> now have a centre of excellence for learning and development . . .
>
> *(Tony Blair, on the website of National School of Government)*

For Pete's sake, Pete, stop encouraging them. Perhaps this is only
partial crap but what you call an elephant is actually a pimple. The
real elephant is government activity itself, fundamentally flawed
because of the impossibility of profit–loss accounting as introduced in
Chapter 8.

In the meantime, the politicos are set on the increasing *censorship* of
prices, energy and carbon emissions being prime examples.

But surely the Lib Dems have a price for pollution. Or do they?

> We will also make sure that the level of penalties that polluters
> have to pay are appropriate to the offence – at present they are
> often trivial; compared with the profits from environmental crime.
>
> *(Liberal Democrats Election Manifesto 2005)*

Environmental crime. We've seen bogus economic crime. What
exactly is environmental crime? Bear in mind that governments led
the way in pollution (and probably still do) by curtailing property
rights in favour of smokestack factories (see Chapter 8). So why can't
the issue be dealt with by property rights including airspace? And how

(and who) are you to calculate the 'appropriate' penalties? Or is that going to come under the Rule of Men?

You're nowhere near as erudite as David Miliband, he of 'one planet, not three' fame:

> Living within the limits of one planet offers the opportunity for a renewal of British food and farming.
>
> *(David Miliband, Labour Party Conference 2006)*

I do like this one, David, I really do. Because apart from condemning poorer countries around the world, possibly to the point of war, this 'renewal' will take up a *lot more land for what is very inefficient energy production.* And this means *less* room for forests to absorb carbon. Come on, brainbox.

But we'll compensate all those food-producing countries for taking away their livelihoods. Aid will come to their aid, won't it, Hilary:

> We will have tripled Britain's aid in a decade; aid that now helps lift more than 5,000 people out of poverty every single day . . .
>
> *(Hilary Benn, Labour Party Conference 2006)*

But the despotic governments ruling most of the world's poor just snaffle your aid; within a day or two it's in Swiss bank accounts. Government-to-government aid doesn't work. I know that, you know that. Or are you telling me that you've aided 5,000 despots?

Or perhaps you've been hooked by Bob Geldof:

> Aid works, aid works.
>
> *(Bob Geldof, Conservative Party Globalisation and Global Party Group,*
> *8 June 2006)*

In that case no doubt you'll be able to explain, Bob, why South Korea, distinctly poorer than Ghana 40 years ago, is now distinctly richer, despite having received no development aid, whilst Ghana, and Africa as a whole, have received whacking great dollops every year in between? (Yes, I know statistics can lie, but who's trying to prove what here? Simple theory and virtually all the evidence are against you Bob.)

'Trade, not aid' is the way to go. The problem is that it's what people want. According to Channel 4's 'After the Tsunami' in January 2005, 'The world's poorer nations increasingly demand "trade not aid".'

What an old-fashioned idea, giving people what they want.

Appendix: Monopolies

What is a monopoly in the private sector, which relies on voluntary purchases and not 'your money or your life'? The typical litmus test for politicos is market share (25 per cent starts the alarm bells). Why? Firstly, what is a 'market'? In other words what product or products are we talking about? Most products do not have discrete and unique features; they overlap with or are similar to other products, or they have substitutes. Every product is unique in some way but every product is dispensable in favour of another. Economist David Friedman (see Chapter 8) argues that he himself is a more typical example of a natural monopoly than is General Motors. As a public speaker, his product is significantly different from any other: 'if you want a certain sort of talk on certain sorts of subjects, you must buy it from me'. F.A. Hayek agreed; size has nothing to do with it.

A classic example of a so-called monopoly was John D Rockefeller's Standard Oil – the cause of the US Anti-Trust Act which now keeps so many politicos like Thomas Barnett in clover. Standard Oil had seen its market share fall from some 90 per cent to under 20 per cent before the Act became law! Again according to Friedman, price-cutting was more often started by the minnows in (often successful) attempts to cut into Standard Oil's market. The manager of one such company remarked later 'it is interesting that most of the ex-Standard employees who testified about Standard's deadly predatory tactics entered the oil business when they left Standard. They also prospered'. The trouble with trying to see off smaller competitors by forcing them to cut prices and make losses is that you inflict the same upon yourself (pro rata) with knobs on; you must also sell at a loss to a huge new market caused by your lower prices.

The chances of a successful cartel are even worse (except when it comes courtesy of Corporatism in the form of government restrictions on competition as described in Chapter 10) because there is an additional temptation to cheat. Yet price-fixing by collusion is a criminal offence.

12

Prolific Crap

It is a far, far better thing to have a firm anchor in nonsense than to put out on the troubled seas of thought.

(J.K. Galbraith)

The backbone of this chapter comes from not so much a double-entry system as a multiple-entry system; several items of crap from the same speech or article, but usually related enough to keep them together. So it's slightly too modest to call them a hotchpotch. Not over-sophisticated, I hope; both writer and reader may be suffering from minor burn-out after the last two chapters in particular.

'Not over-sophisticated' is a good description for our first exhibitor (yes, it's our Dave). And as for the subject matter, after this chapter's opening quotation, where better can one begin than the Farewell State, the primary cause of the fall of Rome. And who better to home in on that than one of its greatest champions, David Cameron, with what must rank as one of the most vacuous of his many vacuous speeches, the Scarman Lecture of 24 November 2006 – a speech on poverty with a poverty of ideas, first and foremost on history.

The acknowledged father of the UK Welfare State was Beveridge whose 1942 report was fully adopted by 1948. (In fact the clearest forerunner was Bismarck whose politics, later much admired by Churchill, were a primary cause of the First World War.) But Dave wants to go back only to 1980. Fishy or what?

Not immediately. For a while, Dave carries on with nothing worse than useless blather (full of 'I want' of course). Thus poverty involves more than the redistribution of money through tax and benefits (not much more, but let's be charitable and assume he's talking about its cure rather than its cause); caused by (ah, here it is) – family break-down, drugs, alcohol, unemployment, poor education. (OK Dave but the Farewell State is responsible for most of these); 'entrenched' poverty reflects lack of supporting structures which help people stand on their own feet. The Conservative mission is to roll forward the frontiers of society. Gordon Brown's Tax and Credit systems are too complex. And so on.

But now he's flexing his muscles for the climax:

> So there is a clear conclusion to the story of poverty and politics over the last twenty-five years. Neither economic liberalism, nor state welfare, are capable of tackling entrenched and persistent poverty.
>
> *(David Cameron, Scarman Lecture 2006)*

As I hope I have made clear, 'economic liberalism' does not describe the UK experience for any part of the last 100 years although there was a brief attempt at starting to dismantle the UK's corporatism, itself copied from Bismarck. And of course total taxes approaching 50 per cent of output are incompatible with any form of liberalism. Slavery describes it better.

Nor does our Dave attempt to back up his assertion. Par.

Here's Dave getting closer to his favourite inanity:

> In place of these things, poverty is the experience of poor housing . . . low educational attainment . . . drug addiction or alcoholism . . . family breakdown . . . and a host of other social forces and factors.
>
> What do all these things have in common? They are all problems that can never be tackled by the state alone. They are social problems – and they require social solutions.
>
> *(David Cameron, Scarman Lecture 2006)*

Ah, 'social' is the key. (Dave has already mentioned his 'Social Justice' group and is getting ready for Social Contracts, both essential to all three main parties back in 1975 – before his 25-year 'look back'.)

Families, Dave, we can understand, even those 'hard-working families' all you politicos go on about – and compel into unemployment due to the minimum wage:

> If we allowed families to decide where the money for childcare went, rather than leaving it up to government . . . we could liberate

many thousands of people from unemployment. I believe passionately that families are the ultimate source of our society's strength or weakness. Families matter because in the end almost every social problem we face comes down to family stability. That's why I've said that I will set a simple test for each and every one of our policies: does it help families? All families do a vital job, and they all need our support.

(David Cameron, Scarman Lecture 2006)

Are we going to see lower taxes as part of this 'help'? We all know the answer. What we are going to see is a change in the paths which taxpayers' money follow, after the initial theft by government:

We need to make sure that local government and the large voluntary groups act less as final recipients of government funding, and more as conduits . . . where there is a level playing field for the voluntary sector to compete with the public and commercial sectors . . . where the funding streams for social enterprise are simplified and longer contracts awarded . . . and where voluntary work is rewarded in the tax and benefits system . . .

I am not naïve or starry-eyed about this big shift – from state to society.

(David Cameron, Scarman Lecture 2006)

In other words a bit of re-routing – to any organizations except businesses, i.e. those who (a) pay tax and (b) can carry out profit–loss calculations. Who is going to pay charities to act as 'conduits'? The taxpayer? This is going to be a humdinger of a fiasco.

This proposal, and my own to return the Farewell State to the charities (see Chapter 6) are like chalk and cheese; firstly our Dave himself wants to be a compulsory 'conduit' with our money, and secondly today's large charities are already compliant conduits; on average the top 500 or so are funded by government to the tune of 40–50 per cent. They are deliverers for the Farewell State, having lost their independence many moons ago.

That's it, folks; Dave's big idea. We shouldn't be surprised:

> For years, we Conservatives talked about rolling back the state. But that is not an end in itself.
>
> *(David Cameron, Scarman Lecture 2006)*

Of course not, David. It's your lifeblood. And our Danegeld.

This looks like a good example of the conduits Dave the Vague has in mind:

> The British Pregnancy Advisory Service, which handles 50,000 terminations a year, is demanding legal reforms to allow abortion on demand as a 'responsible back-up' to contraception . . .
>
> We expect to be in control of our reproductive lives . . .
>
> We feel that it is entirely appropriate for women to have a second chance . . .
>
> *(Ann Furedi, Chief of the BPAS, The Times, 28 November 2006)*

BPAS, responsible for 50 per cent of NHS-funded abortions undertaken by specialist agencies, has not a little interest! And you don't have to be an anti-abortionist to wonder why so many abortions are financed by 'hard-working families' through the NHS, especially when a third of the recipients have had at least one abortion already. And especially when we hear that:

> Making fertility treatment freely available to all would boost Britain's population and help stave off the looming pensions crisis, scientists said yesterday.
>
> Using the latest figures on the costs of fertility treatment, researchers [at Sheffield University] calculated the total value of an IVF baby to the British economy and compared it with a baby conceived naturally.
>
> *(Reported in the Guardian, 20 June, 2006)*

Only a generation ago we were advised by a similar set of fools to have vasectomies to keep the sprog numbers down – I had a power cut in 1972. And I think I got a free radio from the government. And the only looming pensions crisis is Gordon Brown, already responsible off his own bat for some £100 billion plus of company pension scheme losses. Also, under unilateral free trade, Flash, we could keep our savings overseas to be used by young workers for our mutual benefit – we don't need to have many of the young actually living here at all. Perhaps there won't *be* very many if you are promoted!

With any luck, though, some small fraction of this largesse will wend its way, slowly and with many U-turns, to some real live deserving beneficiaries, many of whom will have paid far more in tax already. Of course, how much ends up as cash and not 'in kind' is another matter, but Labour has some plans:

> We will develop personalised budgets in social care where people can decide for themselves what they need and how it should be provided . . .
> We will give older people greater choice over their care. For every older person receiving care or other support, we want to offer transparent, individual budgets which bring funding for a range of services, including social care, care homes, and housing support such as adaptations, maintenance and cleaners together in one place. We will pilot individual budgets for older people by the end of this year.
> *(Labour Party Election Manifesto 2005)*

My mum is 96, and has an Attendance Allowance (although she is not a pilot!). I suppose that explains why a couple of years down the line no budget has dropped out of the sky – anywhere, as far as I can make out. What I can make out is that as reported widely on 11 January 2006, Health Minister Ivan Lewis is telling us that the elderly and disabled will get less care in future. Greater choice over less care!

The Labour Party's great leader still hasn't produced what he wants most of all – a legacy – but in his twilight days he has another go at his favourite false dilemma:

> In a long speech outlining his philosophy on crime, Mr Blair said 'unpalatable choices about liberty and security' needed to be made to 'rebalance' a system in favour of the law-abiding public.
> *(Tony Blair, Guardian Unlimited, 23 June 2006)*

Shame on you, and you a lawyer an' all. No doubt you're thinking of *our* liberty, *your* security. I hope this book has helped to show that liberty *produces* security; invasions of it (at home or abroad) reduce it.

As Ian Loader, a Professor of Criminology, speaking on the same platform, said:

> We have had 25 years of government that have taken law and order very seriously . . . We have had 40 pieces of law and order legislation from this government.
>
> We have had countless new criminal offences, we've got a prison population that is bursting at the seams and we have got sentences in aggregate terms going up not going down.

And when we look at policing, the Victorian era could teach you a few things, Tone, as well as your namesake Ian Blair; appended for interest are the Nine Principles of Policing issued by the Metropolitan Police in 1829.

We mustn't forget that Rowan Williams knows a lot about crime:

> What the victim of crime needs to be sure of is this; that a penalty imposed on the offender is not determined or adjusted for wrong reasons, or corrupt reasons, or because of political pressure or to make a point unconnected with the case.
>
> *(Rowan Williams, Archbishop of Canterbury, reported in the*
> *Daily Telegraph, 29 July 2006)*

Did you take a poll, Rowan? I did, and top of the list was compensation (as was once woven into the system before it was woven out). You may look down your nose at such materialism, but we don't.

And I see you know a lot about prisons:

> The archbishop also urged the Home Secretary to scrap plans for increasing the private sector's role in prisons. 'That the prison service is something for which we take public responsibility, seems to me axiomatic as part of the definition of a just and trustworthy society, and just and trustworthy penal policy,' he said.
>
> 'Franchising, creation of private prisons and private security systems of various kinds, seems to be fraught with problems.'
>
> *(Rowan Williams, Archbishop of Canterbury, reported in the*
> *Daily Telegraph, 29 July 2006)*

Why sniff at private prisons? Is Pentonville private? Er, no:

> Fourteen prison officers were suspended yesterday in a corruption investigation involving the alleged smuggling of mobile phones and drugs into an overcrowded jail.
>
> The men and women suspended from duty at Pentonville prison in North London are also alleged to have had 'inappropriate relations' with inmates. The prison told the courts that it would accept no new inmates for 36 hours.
>
> The prison governor suspended the officers amid allegations that cannabis and mobile phones were being brought in by staff who had become too close to inmates, or had come under pressure from inmates' families.
>
> *(Reported in* The Times*, 15 August 2006)*

And any of the seven prisons referred to below?

> Corruption and drug dealing are rife among staff at seven prisons. A survey leaked to *The Times* reveals that at least 1,200 officers are in the pay of inmates.
>
> *(Reported in* The Times*, 9 September 2006)*

Of course private prisons are not the same thing as private enterprise prisons competing within a genuine market. (No genuine market system would imprison for anything other than direct violence – and if thieves paid victims, they wouldn't need to be overcrowding prisons.) But at least private prisons have profit–loss tests and are likely to be much more efficient – not difficult, Rowan!

Perhaps Rowan's in league with one of Blair's old pals, Michael Barber – a partner in the management consultants McKinsey and Co. and a former head of Blair's 'delivery unit':

> Governments, therefore, face a productivity imperative and three models for meeting this challenge have emerged.
>
> The first is command and control . . .
>
> The second is therefore to create quasi-markets . . .
>
> The third model involves the combination of devolution and transparency . . . Under this model the government contracts with,

or delegates to, service providers and holds them accountable.

Many public sector reforms around the world combine elements of the three models.

(Michael Barber, The Times, *27 September 2006)*

Again, anything except privatization and profit–loss disciplines.

Management consultants are renowned for borrowing your watch to tell you the time but as government advisers spending your money their scope is limitless; well over £2 billion a year in the UK (that we know about!).

Government just chooses not to get it, and as for 'law and order, on the other hand, the state provides for the public good' (see Chapter 8) the irony would be lost – despite the fact that, like private security services, private sector law services are increasingly a major feature of life. Especially in the US, where arbitration and alternative dispute resolution (ADR) services have made the courts a secondary recourse in many areas and completely superfluous in others.

Yet both there and here the state encroaches further. We touched on 'Goldilocks' in the previous chapter, in which government agencies know and impose the exact prices companies should 'charge', as if consumers are gasping for advice and can't vote with their feet. Now that really is fascism. As R.W. Grant has pointed out for us, you can be done either way – a bit higher than Goldilocks and you're 'gouging', a bit lower and you're a 'predator' in a 'price war'.

So it's not surprising that sometimes you're *ordered* to raise your prices (and reduce consumer satisfaction as well as your own). Despite 'the myth of integrated planning', there is a Commission for Integrated Transport – which wants to go after supermarkets for other reasons – especially with eco-warriors on the warpath:

Free parking at out-of-town shopping centres must be abolished to save traditional high streets from terminal decline and protect the environment, a government commission will recommend today.

The Commission for Integrated Transport believes that the lack of parking fees at centres such as Lakeside in Essex and Meadowhall in Sheffield is causing shoppers to use their cars and desert towns and cities.

It proposes that centres are forced to charge for parking and spend the money on better bus services and access for pedestrians and cyclists.

(Reported in The Times, *19 July 2006)*

Got you by the short and curlies. You can't get round it by knocking prices off the goods instead. All must pay for an NHS 'free at the point of use' but shoppers can't park free at the point of use unless Big Brother chooses the points of use.

We the sheeple will have just got used to this when the U-turn comes (perhaps because the eco-warriors have been rumbled, having destroyed and terminated millions of lives in the process). Whatever.

No doubt it will be too late by then to help the prescient Joss Bolton who wrote to *The Times* on 21 July 2006:

> I have not been to a town centre to shop for years. Poor choice, limited parking and terrible congestion are among the reasons. A visit to Bluewater or Lakeside, carefully planned, can take care of my needs for months.
>
> Perhaps the quango should have looked at the evolving nature of our town centres, and promote the change to residential, eating and drinking.

Careful, Joss. Free speech no longer applies under the Rule of Men – or Women, not least Margaret Beckett who would already have you muzzled as a terrorist (see Chapter 7).

And at present the eco-warriors remain the warlords – often in the Fourth Estate:

> British supermarkets used to shower free plastic bags on their customers. They saved time at the checkout and identified goods that had been paid for. Now the environmentally aware stores ask customers whether they want a plastic bag, in tones inviting the answer 'No'.
>
> It will take time to re-educate the planet to environmentally unselfish behaviour. Sticks and carrots are needed, and above all, education and sensitive intelligence. But, paradoxically, the plastic bag is a simple place to start.
>
> *(The Times, leading article 11 November 2006)*

Perhaps the planet's re-education should start with its size compared to a person or a plastic bag. You could put everyone in the world into a suitably shaped cuboid box with a volume of about one cubic mile, and dump it in Lake Superior to be sunk without a ripple or trace for evermore. And then think about plastic bags. You mean that kind of re-education? Or the virtues of private property to solve Garrett Hardin's tragedy of the commons (see Chapter 6)? I'm all in favour of that.

Does Janice Turner know that? Writing on the same day (National Eco-Warriors' Day and if not why not?) she says we are all green self-deceivers:

> Who could not smile grimly at *The Times* front-page report this week that showed the gulf about how green we claim to be and how we actually live? For example, 75 per cent of us say we avoid unnecessary car journeys and yet millions more miles are driven every year.
>
> *(Janice Turner, The Times, 11 November 2006)*

Who are *we*, Janice? Most of us may well be green self-deceivers, by refusing to accept that the politicos are conning us, not re-educating us, with pseudo-scientific mumbo-jumbo – your colleague Libby Purves would probably call it philosophy (see Chapter 2). The philosophy is simple – use mumbo-jumbo to tell people the earth is flat and with any luck you'll get a run of as much as a century *after* the theory has been blown wide-open. All you need is Big Government, state education, academic tenure rules (by which the current big idea is regularly reinforced through peer-reviewed tosh) and off you go.

But one fine day, if private enterprise is not fully banned, there'll not only be private collection of bags and rubbish, but private depositing of rubbish on *another* planet, in the process making David Miliband's one planet look a bit sick.

In the meantime private enterprise on this planet is being strangled, at an alarming speed, both physically and by indoctrination. Here's another journo gone west – to New Orleans to be precise:

> George W. Bush and Mr Nagin seem to agree on one thing: that the market will put everything right in the devastated city. But that is a

view as blind and as indiscriminate as Katrina itself. The governments of east Africa could tell them that the market will not right humanitarian disaster – it will only exploit it.

Messrs. Bush and Nagin have spent the last year getting it wrong

. . .

Poor New Orleans. An act of God is one thing, but the inaction of government is another.

(Andrew O'Hagan, Daily Telegraph, *30 August 2006)*

The sheer ignorance on display here, not only of the meaning of markets versus government but also of the roles played by each in this catastrophe, is truly frightening, especially in the *Daily Telegraph*.

Yes, Katrina was an act of God, but the breaking of the levees (which was the major cause of the disaster) was not. It was an act of government (in the shape of the Army Corps of Engineers) failing to maintain *its own property*, the history of which is well documented following the previous flood in 1999.

George Bush does NOT believe in free markets; he is an apostle for big government linked with big companies. (Ever heard of Halliburton?)

Government had indeed 'spent the last year getting it wrong' – from day one, when after issuing a warning to residents, most of the officials packed their bags and went to the safety of Baton Rouge. (Let's go, chaps.) The relief operation, which can be measured in $ billions was steeped in theft and fraud – from bogus Social Security numbers to police joining in the looting, as well as pushing around innocents and corralling them into places like the Superdrome under house arrest.

Far more importantly, government physically stopped markets from helping out. For example it prevented Coast Guards from delivering fuel and the Red Cross from delivering food. It blocked a huge flotilla from delivering aid, and it blocked Wal-Mart from delivering water.

Ah, Wal-Mart, the unsung hero which, while FEMA (Federal Emergency Management Agency) was shooting off memos, offered $20 million in cash, 1500 truckloads of free merchandise and food for 100,000 meals. As economist Christopher Westley wrote, FEMA should be abolished. 'Wal-mart is far from the only over-taxed firm trying to provide it [good business] along the Gulf Coast, reflecting the naturally cooperative relationship between producers and consumers'.[1]

Perhaps I could have spared you most of this by simply referring to one phrase of Andrew O'Hagan's piece: 'The people of Thailand and Sumatra will tell them that capital aid that is properly managed and applied will lead not only to human recovery but the recovery of the market too.' But there too, Andrew, governments hindered rather than helped the operation. And what markets are we talking about in east Africa, pray? Next thing, you'll soon be telling us that the 'botched' reconstruction of Iraq was the fault of markets.

Speaking of which, Donald Rumsfeld has been eliminated from the scene of battle – as George Bush prepares to step it up again – but it would be a shame not to mark his passing with a few of his pearls of wisdom, courtesy of *The Times*:

On the location of WMDs: 'We know where they are. They're in the area around Tikrit and Baghdad and east, west, south, and north somewhat.' (30 March 2003)

'The absence of evidence is not evidence of absence.' (June 2002)

'I can't tell you if the use of force in Iraq will last five days, five weeks or five months, but it won't last any longer than that.' (November 2002)

'I don't do quagmires.' (July 2003)

---

1 Christopher Westley, Mises Institute, 12 September 2005.

On disorder in Iraq: 'Stuff happens.' (April 2003)

More on disorder in Iraq: 'It's untidy, and freedom's untidy. Free people are free to make mistakes and commit crimes and do bad things. They're also free to live their lives and do wonderful things.' (April 2003)

On his unwillingness to talk about coalition dead: 'Death has a tendency to encourage a depressing view of war.' (May 2003)

'If you are not criticized, you may not be doing much.' One of 'Rumsfeld's Rules'.

(Donald Rumsfeld, reported in The Times, *14 April 2006)*

Seems a bit mean not to say bye-bye to George:

The evil that inspired and rejoiced in 9/11 is still at work in the world. And so long as that's the case, America is still a nation at war.

(George Bush, State of the Union Address, 23 January 2007)

Great message, George. Centuries of war to look forward to. But then as Randolph Bourne said, 'War is the health of the state'.

In the other direction, over the North Sea to Europe, there are also madcap plans – about wine lakes. The trouble is that Authority doesn't know whether the wine should be drunk or conjured into fuel:

The unquenchable desire of Britons for New World wines has forced Brussels to order nearly a billion bottles of French and Italian wine to be turned into fuel and disinfectant. The European Commission will then spend €2.4 billion (£1.65 billion) digging up vineyards across the continent.

Under the Common Agricultural Policy, the farmers will then be paid for not producing wine but for keeping up environmental standards on their land instead. Brussels, which for years paid people to set up vineyards, believes there are now too many small-scale wine-makers producing poor wine, and that the industry needs to consolidate. In France, there is one worker per hectare of vineyards; in Australia, one worker for every 50 hectares.

*(*The Times, *8 June 2006)*

Another short and curlies job here; once they've got your money they're going to spend it; giving it back isn't in the Rule of Men.

But there is only one way to wind up the last chapter of this book – back in the UK and into politics.

First of all I'd like to say goodbye to Ruth Kelly who does what she does best – sets up commissions:

> Welcome – and thanks to all of you who have come here today to launch the Commission on Integration and Cohesion . . .
>
> I believe this is why we have moved from a period of uniform consensus on the value of multiculturalism, to one where we can encourage that debate by questioning whether it is encouraging separateness.
>
> *(Ruth Kelly, at launch of Commission on Integration and Cohesion,*
> *24 August 2006)*

We were force-fed into 'multi-culturalism' (to the point where a headmaster, Ray Honeyford, was sacked for daring to wonder about this creed in 1984). Now we're to be force-fed into something else; once again, the principle is 'force' – the direction of it doesn't really matter. And have no doubt, the Commission, dominated by politicians, will come up with force as a solution. Extract funds by force, impose obedience by force:

> It is our responsibility to make sure that the Commission can engage with the latest and most innovative policy interventions.
>
> *(Ruth Kelly, at launch of Commission on Integration and Cohesion,*
> *24 August 2006)*

Hardly smacks of liberation does it?

But the journo-politicos are up there with the best on chutzpah. We can move from multi-culturism to multi-people crap:

> Mr Clarke is probably the most experienced, articulate, dynamic and morally unimpeachable Labour politician after Mr Blair himself and Gordon Brown.
>
> *(Anatole Kaletsky, The Times, 4 May 2006)*

Well it can't be tongue-in-cheek; Kaletsky doesn't do tongue-in-cheek.

But as we saw in Chapter 10 he does do a whiff of Marx occasionally. He's not alone; in mid 2005 a BBC audience voted Marx as their top philosopher. This is the man who held that a worker spending an hour digging a hole and filling it up again should be paid for the hour irrespective of the result. (Hey, sounds good – how about paying me £100 an hour for writing this book, even if sales are zero? All I need is a Marxist publisher – damn, too late.)

I think I'll stop paying my licence fee. Oh sorry I can't – that 'force' thing keeps getting in the way.

Another Marxist nonsense concerned time-preference, more correctly the lack of it (see Chapter 11). But to even talk of time-preference is 'racist' in the land of the free – or at least in Seattle:

> Are you salting away a little money for your retirement? Trying to plan for your kids' education? If so, Seattle Public Schools seems to think you're a racist.
>
> According to the district's official Web site, 'having a future time orientation' (academese for having long-term goals) is among the 'aspects of society that overtly and covertly attribute value and normality to white people and Whiteness, and devalue, stereotype and label people of colour.'
>
> *(Andrew J Coulson, CATO Institute publication, 2 June 2006)*

And left to the last – another politico at *The Times*, occasionally seen amongst the Tories, Daniel Finkelstein:

> Policymaking, then, is a bit of a con. Manifestos pretend to be an entire programme for government when in reality even the most detailed of them only cover a few items. Voters don't make judgments based on these programmes and they shouldn't either.
>
> What matters is not such bogus 'substance', it is the governing style of the prospective rulers. Are they strong or weak? Interferers or liberals? Atlanticists or Europhiles? Moderates or extremists? Localisers or centralisers? Tax cutters or big spenders? Tied to vested interests or independent of them? Free traders or protectionists? In touch or out of touch? These are the sort of questions voters should ask . . .

Labour has spent much of the past five years undoing stupid things it committed itself to in opposition and then did in its first five years. The problem with politicians, you see, is not that they don't do what they say they will, but the opposite – they try to do what they said they would do, even after realising it wasn't a good plan.

(Daniel Finkelstein, The Times, *4 October 2006)*

A manifesto 'pretends' – true. Voters 'don't make judgments' on them – true. So why bother? Try pretending in a company prospectus and then try and stay out of jail.

Substance is 'bogus', what counts is 'style' – in a number of areas that are actually full of substance! Here are the answers to your questions, Fink, on the 'style' of all three major parties:

Preferably weak. Interferers. Both. Extremists. Centralizers. Big Spenders. Tied to vested interests. Protectionists. Out of touch.

If voters are genuinely interested in the answers, they know there is nothing to choose and will vote on 'what's in it for me'. If they aren't interested (perfectly rationally) they'll also vote on 'what's in it for me' – or won't vote at all (also perfectly rational – whoever you vote for, it doesn't count and Big Government gets in).

And as for politicians 'trying to do what they said they would do', Fink, I'm speechless. Well not quite. Yes, they know it's not a good plan and as soon as they're in power they jettison it – in favour of a worse one. If they see this behaviour in others, even in relatively mild form, they call it perverting the course of justice. 'The problem with politicos, you see', Fink, is that like those in Orwell's *Animal Farm*, they want to enslave and milk the sheeple.

Appendix

The Nine Principles of Policing (issued by the Metropolitan Police in 1829)

1. To prevent crime and disorder, as an alternative to their repression by military force and severity of legal punishment.
2. To recognise always that the power of the police to fulfil their duties is dependent on public approval of their existence, actions and behaviour and on their ability to secure and maintain public respect.

3. To recognise always that to secure and maintain the respect and approval of the public means also the securing of the willing co-operation of the public in the task of securing observance of laws.

4. To recognise always that the extent to which the co-operation of the public can be secured diminishes proportionately the necessity of the use of physical force and compulsion for achieving police objectives.

5. To seek and preserve public favour, not by pandering to public opinion; but by constantly demonstrating absolutely impartial service to law, in complete independence of policy, and without regard to the justice or injustice of the substance of individual laws, by ready offering of individual service and friendship to all members of the public without regard to their wealth and social standing, by ready exercise of courtesy and friendly good humour; and by ready offering of individual sacrifice in protecting and preserving life.

6. To use physical force only when the exercise of persuasion, advice and warning is found to be insufficient to obtain public co-operation to an extent necessary to secure observance of law to restore order, and to use only the minimum degree of physical force which is necessary on any particular occasion for achieving a police objective.

7. To maintain at all times a relationship with the public that gives reality to the historic tradition that the police are the public and the public are the police. The police being only members of the public who are paid to give full-time attention to duties which are incumbent on every citizen in the interest of community welfare and existence.

8. To recognise always the need for strict adherence to police-executive functions, and to refrain from even seeming to usurp the powers of the judiciary or avenging individuals or the State, and of authoritatively judging guilt and punishing the guilty.

9. To recognise always that the test of police efficiency is the absence of crime and disorder, and not the visible evidence of police action in dealing with them.

Conclusion

> *A democracy cannot exist as a permanent form of government. It can only exist until a majority of voters discover that they can vote themselves largess out of the public treasury.*
>
> *(Alexander Fraser Tytler, 1787)*

In other words democracy evolves into kleptocracy – and we're approaching the end-game. The greater the power of politicians, the more that particular 'calling' attracts charlatans and control freaks, usually both. As P.J. O'Rourke has said, if government were a product, selling it would be illegal. I hope that this book has provided some justification for that remark, and a few chuckles as well.

The relentless rise of political power is indisputable, the logical end being that, as mentioned in Chapter 11, everything is either banned or compulsory, and all under the Hazel Blears' banner (excuse the pun) of democracy, in which theft is permitted provided you use government as the middle man.

The problem is the power, not the stripes of those who wield it.

During the end-game, the politicos become shriller and shriller. Voting is your duty; the 40 per cent who don't participate in an elective dictatorship are guilty of apathy – a mortal sin. But when the forty per cent becomes fifty, sixty, and more, and they have to cope with a demonstration or two, perhaps they'll catch on.

A better way is to register serious discontent. As I advocated in the first edition, go to the voting booth, tick the box 'none-of-the-above' if you're lucky enough to have one, otherwise cross out the lot, with a rude message. Nothing apathetic about that, although I'm told that in the latter case your vote will not be counted. Go on, you have nothing to lose but your chains.

Index of Names

Aaronovitch, David 66, 74, 75
Abbot, Isabella 146
Ainsworth, Peter 35, 127
Alexander, Douglas 91
Armstrong, Hilary 44
Association of Convenience
    Stores 127

Baker, Gerard 65
Barber, Michael 159
Barnett, Thomas (US) 149
Barroso, Jose-Manuel (EU)
    62, 102
Beattie, Liz 14
Beckett, Margaret 6, 28, 29,
    34, 90
Benn, Hilary 151
Blair, Sir Ian 19, 30, 112
Blair, Tony 41, 43, 54, 104,
    109, 112, 150, 157
Blears, Hazel 10, 61, 76
Brown, Gordon 38, 39, 53, 90,
    104, 138, 139
Bush, George W (US) 13, 23,
    56, 57 (et al), 100, 115, 119
    (et al), 165
Butler, Tom 144
Byers, Stephen 34

Cable, Vincent 27
Callaghan, James 16
Cameron, David 8, 21, 31, 32,
    52, 71, 88, 128, 140, 154–6
Campbell, Sir Menzies 6, 7, 31
Carmichael, Alistair 76
Challen, Colin 103
Clarke, Charles 13, 90
Clarke, Peter 112
Conservative Party 6, 8, 9, 11,
    12, 19, 51, 71, 81, 85, 86, 98
Constantine, Rowland 96
Cooper, Yvette 33, 113

Dahrendorf, Ralf 5, 94
Darling, Alistair 20, 77, 89
Davis, David 35, 52
Democratic Party (US) 12, 23,
    24, 86, 89, 101
Dodge, Toby (re EU, UN) 27

Edwards, Lynn 131
European Union (EU) 48, 165

Fabian Society 99
Fahy, Peter 72
Falconer, Charles (Lord
    Falconer) 110
Finkelstein, Daniel 167

Fowler, Neil 147
Furedi, Ann 156

Geldof, Bob 151
Godson, Dean 142
Goldsmith, Peter (Lord Goldsmith) 109
Grayling, Chris 20
Guardian, The 38, 65

Hain, Peter 26, 81
Harding, James 140
Harris et al (US) 91
Hastert & Frist (US) 148
Hattersley, Roy 5
Healey, Denis 38
Heath, Ted 80
Heseltine, Michael 25
Hewitt, Patricia 14, 41, 54, 70, 88
Higgins, John 124
Holliday, Steve 124
Home Office (Study on rape) 122
Hoon, Geoff 131
Hughes, Beverley 70
Huhne, Chris 55
Hutton, John 114

Johnson, Alan 43, 69, 84
Jowell, Tessa 32, 116

Kaletsky, Anatole 95, 134, 145, 146, 166
Kelly, Ruth 29, 43, 60, 82, 83, 98, 166

Kerry, John 23
Kroes, Ms Neelie (EU) 117

Labour Party 10, 11, 18, 26, 30, 31, 40, 42, 47, 50, 53, 54, 56, 72, 73, 85, 86, 99, 105, 106, 129, 130, 157
Lammy, David 96
Lane, Geoffrey (Lord Justice Lane) 121
Liberal Democrats 7, 17, 53, 75, 82, 87, 150
Livingstone, Ken 22, 60

Malloch Brown, Sir Mark 118
Mandelson, Peter 139
Maude, Francis 94
Meacher, Michael 141
Miliband, David 10, 129, 151
Millward, David 51
Mora, Camilo 68
Murphy, Paul 111

Nazir-Ali, Michael 132
North Wales Police 30

O'Hagan, Andrew 162
Osborne, George 20

Prescott, John 59
Purves, Libby 21, 111

Rammell, Bill 42
Raphael, Adam 18
Reid, John 18, 90

Republican Party (US)   118

Riddell, Peter   59, 135, 149, 150

Rumsfeld, Donald (US)   164–5

Seattle Public Schools (US)   167

Spelman, Caroline   8, 9

Straw, Jack   58, 59

Syed, Matthew   125

Taylor, Sir Cyril   96

Teather, Sarah   29, 46

Thomas, Harford   65, 144

Thorpe, Jeremy (Liberal Party)   16

Times, The   49, 122, 161

Turner, Janice   162

United Nations (UN)   118, 143

Vanhanen, Matti (EU)   63

Walker, Peter   80

Warner, Norman (Lord Warner)   116, 133

Wicks, Malcolm   102

Willetts, David   17

Williams, Rowan   29, 158

Williams, Venus   147

Wilmott, Steve   110

Woolas, Phil   113

Subject Index

Big Government (including planning) 1, 2, 3, 67, 94, 95, 99–102, 105–7, 135, 160–1, 170

Corporatism/ State Regulation 3, 51, 124–7, 154–6
Crime (and victims) 18–19, 30, 47–8, 58, 72–3, 121–3, 158–9, 168–9

Democracy 12–13, 60–1, 135–6, 170
Disasters 162–4

Economics 137–52
Education 29, 42–4, 49, 69–72, 81–4, 96–7, 130–2
Environment and Energy 20, 34–5, 55–6, 65–8, 77–8, 89–90, 100–3, 128–30, 150–1, 161–2

Iraq 3, 12, 23, 27, 56, 73–4, 104, 115, 164–5

Liberties and Security 13–14, 57–8, 73–4, 91, 112–13, 117, 123, 132, 157–8

National Health Service (NHS) etc. 11, 39–42, 53–4, 70–1, 98, 107, 125–6, 144, 156

Socialism and Political Spectrum 10, 94, 134

Taxation 6–8, 19–20, 37–8, 46, 48–9, 75–80, 85–8, 91–2, 134, 154–5
Trade and Movement (Freedom of) 49, 79, 94, 138–43, 151–2

War and Terrorism 1, 13, 23, 28, 56, 58, 62, 67, 73–5, 104 (*see also* Trade and Movement) 138, 165
Welfare State 1, 44–6, 53, 76–7, 84, 86, 115, 141, 153–7